# MYTHOLOGY AND THE TOLERANCE
# OF THE JAVANESE

BENEDICT R. O'G. ANDERSON

# MYTHOLOGY AND THE TOLERANCE OF THE JAVANESE

EQUINOX
PUBLISHING
JAKARTA   KUALA LUMPUR

Equinox Publishing (Asia) Pte Ltd
No 3. Shenton Way
#10-05 Shenton House
Singapore 068805

www.EquinoxPublishing.com


Mythology and the Tolerance of the Javanese
by Benedict R. O'G. Anderson


ISBN 978-602-8397-37-7


First Equinox Edition 2009


Copyright © 1965,1996 Cornell Modern Indonesia Project
640 Stewart Avenue, Ithaca, NY 14850-3857
Cornell Modern Indonesia Project No. 37
Reprinted 2004.


Printed in the United States


1 3 5 7 9 10 8 6 4 2

# PREFACE

All of those who are interested in contemporary Indonesian society, its organization and social and political articulation, sooner or later come to realize that in order to achieve any real depth of understanding for these phenomena it is first necessary to appreciate the enduring and frequently manifest residuum of traditional, pre-Western culture in Indonesia. Certainly this is true with respect to Java, whose culture has of course had an impact far beyond the shores of that island. In many cases these legacies of traditional culture help to explain current phenomena; in addition they make much more understandable the Javanese approach to religion—not only to Islam but also to Hinduism and Buddhism, which were introduced to the island earlier. For they have conditioned the way in which all outside ideas, Western and non-Western, have been received, and they help to account for the particular patterns of synthesis which are woven into the Javanese *milieu*. Most striking is the way in which persisting elements of old Javanese culture affect contemporary values. An ability to accommodate to and tolerate conflicting norms and ideas, the capacity to entertain in coexistence ideas and values that would seem incompatible in many Western settings, an unusual capacity for sympathetic toleration in social behavior—these are all attributes of contemporary Javanese society deriving from old Javanese culture.

For the outsider, such elements are probably most easily approached and understood through the traditional artistic medium of the *wayang*—the Javanese shadowplays based upon adaptations and developments of major themes and episodes in the Ramayana and the Mahabharata. These *wayang* plays, performed with flat leather puppets which throw their sharply etched shadows against a screen which is viewed from the other side, are as important a part of contemporary Javanese culture as they were of the old.

To discern this relationship between the *wayang* plays and Javanese society, to achieve an insight into the values which have been conveyed by *wayang* over the centuries, and then to perceive these patterns of social conduct and morality in a dynamic phase of interaction and adjustment with the new values and social concepts born in Indonesia of the Japanese occupation, the Revolution, and the rapid change of a post-revolutionary society, is an accomplishment few non-Indonesians would be capable of. Nor, indeed, would it be possible for most Indonesians, for their involvement in the culture and the society is so close that they miss the perspective necessary to appraise and describe these phenomena to an outside audience.

Mr. Benedict Anderson's study of the *wayang* and its sociological and psychological significance is, I believe, a real contribution to our understanding of Javanese culture and values. A political scientist by training (he has recently returned from Indonesia after three years of research there, primarily on the Revolutionary period), he has long been interested in Javanese art, drama, and music and has achieved unusually deep insights into these aspects of the Javanese civilization. Mr. Anderson wishes to emphasize that this study is exploratory in nature and that the conclusions he reaches are tentative. He would welcome comments and criticism on the material he is presenting.

George McT. Kahin
Director

Ithaca, New York
August 24, 1965

# TABLE OF CONTENTS

# LIST OF ILLUSTRATIONS

These illustrations are drawn from J. Kats, *Het Javaansche Tooneel, I, Wajang Purwa*, Weltevreden, 1923, and Hardjowirogo, *Sedjarah Wajang Purwa*, Perpustakaan Perguruan Kementerian P. P. & K., Djakarta, 1955. For technical reasons, it has not proved possible to reproduce them all to scale.

# INTRODUCTION

I would like to make it clear that the following essay is essentially exploratory, designed to raise certain questions about Javanese culture and values. The main idea has been to take *wayang* out of the framework of drama and literary studies in which it has traditionally been confined and try to put it in a wider sociological and psychological context, to see what clues it may provide for a deeper understanding of Javanese society. What I have said is in no sense to be taken as anything more than a preliminary and very incomplete attempt to explain a small part of this vast subject. I am aware that many opinions and judgments have been expressed with what will seem to be excessive assertiveness and perhaps unnecessary acerbity, but this has been done at least partly on purpose, in the hope thereby of arousing interest and discussion in an area of Indonesia studies largely neglected in our time. I realize only too well the superficiality of my own knowledge of the immense complexities of Javanese civilization and can therefore only hope that the inadequacies of this essay will earn at least the tolerance of Indonesian readers.

Some of the basic ideas of this essay I owe to talks in Djakarta with Professor G. J. Resink in 1964, though it goes without saying that anything said here is entirely my own responsibility. I would like to acknowledge with gratitude the help of Mrs. Claire Holt, Mrs. Arlene Lev, Mr. N. Tirtaamidjaja, and Mr. Pandam Guritno Siswoharsojo, who read parts of the text and made many invaluable suggestions. I would like also to thank Mrs. Susan Finch for her contribution towards whatever order and clarity the final version of this manuscript has.

Benedict R. O'G. Anderson

Ithaca, New York
August 7, 1965

# MYTHOLOGY
# AND THE
# TOLERANCE OF THE JAVANESE

## I

Most Europeans and Americans who have lived long in Java sooner or later fall under the spell of her ancient civilization. Yet the specific quality of Javanese life and culture which impresses the foreigner seems regularly to elude description. In earlier decades observers were fond of referring to "Javanese syncretism" and the "Javanese sense of relativism." But especially since the outbreak of Indonesia's national revolution, it has become popular to speak of the "tolerance" of the Javanese as their quintessential characteristic. Whether or not the Javanese themselves traditionally regarded tolerance as one of their salient ethnic traits, nowadays they too are likely to take a quiet pride in their reputation for broadmindedness and *savoir vivre*.

The growing unanimity of devoted foreigners and of the educated Javanese on the wide prevalence of tolerance in Javanese society can be accounted for by a large number of psychological, political, and historical factors which need not concern us here. Nonetheless this unanimity has tended to shield the idea of Javanese tolerance from even friendly scrutiny and analysis. It is therefore the hope of shedding some light on the concrete social and cultural aspects of this "tolerance" that guides the highly tentative discussion that follows.

## II

It should be said first of all that the "Javanese sense of relativism" should in no sense be understood as a generalized tolerance of differences regardless of race, color, or creed. It does not, as a rule, extend unconditionally to the other ethnic groups in Indonesia, to whom the Javanese normally feel a little superior. Nor does it include the Chinese and Europeans, the other significant alien groups in Java. Both these communities wear an ambiguous prestige, inherited from the colonial age. The Javanese advise against marriage with Chinese, observing that "their ashes are older"—in other words, that the children are likely to prove more Chinese than Javanese. Yet certainly the Chinese are more generally accepted in Javanese society than, for example, among the Sundanese. But this is largely because Chinese settlement in Central and East Java goes back for many generations, and the local Chinese have largely assimilated to Javanese culture. In the Priangan, from which the Chinese were barred till the early part of this century, immigration is new; and the clash of contrasting cultures still stirs enmity and distrust. As for the Americans and Europeans, even today they profit from the residues of colonial racism. White visitors, especially those from the intellectual and official class, are usually treated with high deference. Eccentricities are accepted gracefully, but as part of an alien order without direct relevance for Javanese life.

If, then, tolerance is not strikingly evident in the relationships of the Javanese with outsiders, in what does it consist? What do the Javanese themselves have in mind when they speak of this characteristic of their culture? There can be little doubt that for the average Javanese the idea of *toleransi,* as such, is inextricably associated with the peculiar nature of religion in Java. Somewhere at the back (or front) of his mind will be lurking the problem of his relationship to Islam. A typical Javanese formulation might well be: "Of course I am a Moslem, but not a fanatical Moslem like the Atjehnese. We Javanese can get along with Christians and Buddhists. We see truth in all religions and are not exclusive in our beliefs."

Yet behind this theological broadmindedness and rational sophistication there is evident a certain disingenuousness. For the fact is that though the Javanese are overwhelmingly an Islamic people on paper, the real spiritual commitment of the great majority to this religion is little more than nominal. The voting strength of the confessional Islamic parties on Java is to be found primarily among the alien Sundanese of West Java and the Madurese of Madura and the Oosthoek. Islam among the ethnic Javanese is strongest in the commercial townships of the Pasisir (North coast), which historically have been most influenced by foreign cultures— Chinese, Arabic, and European—and which, politically and socially, are most remote from the geographic heartland of Javanese civilization in South Central Java. Since a majority of Javanese do not feel themselves to be Islamic in any profound sense, their tolerance of non-Islamic religious beliefs is scarcely a matter of high principle. In many cases it is simply a useful defense against the political and moral claims of an aggressive and orthodox Islamic minority. In the classical opposition within Javanese communities between *santri* (committed Islamic) and *abangan* (nominally Islamic) groups, "tolerance" is basically a weapon to deny ascendancy to the *santri* and assure the continued legitimacy of traditional *abangan* domination.

This becomes all the clearer when one looks at the attitude of many *abangan* Javanese towards Christianity. In various areas of East and Central Java, Protestant and Catholic sects have played an important historical role. Like Islam, Christianity offered a release for those who suffered too cruelly from the frustrations generated by a static, traditional society. Becoming a Christian removed a man from the established hierarchies of the Javanese community, in which rank and religion were inextricably intertwined since the highest spiritual powers were attributed to the temporal rulers of Java, such as the Susuhunan of Surakarta and the Sultan of Jogjakarta. Of the rival Christian sects, it has been the Catholics who have made the most spectacular progress in Java, since their clergy are mostly Javanese, and they have generally shown a sophisticated willingness to make the necessary adjustments to traditional Javanese ideas and prejudices.

Nevertheless, there has always been an inescapable loss of caste involved in a Javanese becoming a Christian. In the colonial period, to be sure, Javanese Christians won a certain position in the community through sharing a religion with their colonial rulers. Since the revolution, this ambiguous prestige has naturally vanished. But it is not simply the previous colonial associations which underlie the widespread feeling that Javanese Christians, even Javanese Catholics, do not really belong to the Javanese family in the fullest sense. Like the strongly Islamic *santris,* Christians are felt to threaten the stability of the traditional order by making claims to social honor which cannot be justified within that order. Such feelings tend to be especially strong at the present time, when the grave problems of Javanese and even Indonesian identity are intimately bound up with the disintegration of traditional society.

Even in the strictly theological sphere, Christianity usually wins approval only in a very limited sense. The Javanese sees "truth," but not "the truth," in all religions. In other words, he looks for and approves those Christian ideas which are felt to be *tjotjog* (in harmony) with the Javanese *weltanschauung*. The rest are completely ignored. Christianity is valid to the extent that it approximates to the Javanese religion.

Many non-Christian Javanese send their children to the excellent Catholic schools in the larger cities. But it is usually with the firm, if unstated, understanding that they will not become Catholics. The schools are popular insofar as they offer access to the secular Western education which is increasingly the *sine qua non* of social mobility and an honorable career.

Christianity, then, and particularly its Catholic variant, is tolerated for quite specific social and political reasons. In institutional form it offers a widely respected means of access to modernity; as a religious organization it provides a highly respectable pretext for fending off the political, social, and moral claims of orthodox Islam. Where Christianity acquires prestige in itself, it is insofar as it conforms to a Javanese ethos and a Javanese conception of life.

Another illustration of the Javanese idea of religious tolerance is the Javanese attitude towards Buddhism. On Java, the Buddhists are a very small group indeed; yet they have considerable prestige for a variety of reasons. Their numbers are drawn almost exclusively from metropolitan and provincial elite circles—high army officers, government officials, and wealthy, established Chinese. Moreover, in the collective Javanese memory Buddhism is associated with the Tantric religion of the pre-Islamic epoch in which the great Javanese empire of Modjopahit reached the apogee of its glory. The fact that Modjopahit was finally humbled by a coalition of North coast Islamic states, led by Demak, ushering in the so-called Dark Ages of Javanese history and eventually Dutch colonial rule, is nowhere forgotten. For the largely *abangan* Javanese ruling class, which is pleased to trace its political and familial ancestry back to Modjopahit, an ill-defined "Buddhism" has thus very favorable connotations. Moreover, in the traditionalist *abangan* religious culture, which has been engaged in an ill-concealed competition with Islam for many centuries, there are undoubtedly still existent many Tantric Buddhist-derived elements.

Yet on the other hand, the Balinese religion, which also contains Buddhist as well as Hindu (Shivaitic) and animist elements and probably approximates reasonably closely to the historical Tantric religion of Modjopahit, is regarded with scant respect. It is clear that this is because the Javanese, as an ethnic group, look upon the Balinese and their way of life as *kasar* (coarse), *ramé* (noisy), and *désa* (peasant, primitive). To this day, the *agama Bali* (Balinese religion) has not been accorded full recognition by the Javanese-dominated government in Djakarta.

In brief, the crucial factors to be taken into account if one is assessing the degree of real religious tolerance in any particular case are the ethnic and class associations of the relevant religious group. One should not argue that the Javanese are tolerant of Christianity and "Buddhism" as such, but insofar as these religious systems have been assimilated to "Javanism" and to the extent that their adherents are respectable Javanese.

### III

It may appear from the foregoing discussion that what has been widely regarded as an admirable broadmindedness among the Javanese is simply a rather subtle form of cultural chauvinism. Yet in fact nothing could be further from the truth. But only when certain generalized misconceptions have been dispelled can one perceive clearly the real and, it seems to me, admirably wide dimensions of the Javanese respect for human variety. For the real character of Javanese "tolerance" should be sought not in any abstract "humanist" acceptance of conflicting ethical or religious systems, but rather in the Javanese people's sense of their own personality and traditions. The immense strength of Javanese cultural self-consciousness is illustrated by the fact that immature children are said to be *durung Djåwå*—"not yet Javanese"— rather than, as we might put it, "not yet adult." But it is just this proud self-confidence which forms the emotional and psychological underpinning for the "real" Javanese tolerance. So deeply ingrained is this pride that almost anything is tolerated, provided that it can be adapted to or explained in terms of the Javanese way of life.

One of the most striking contrasts between Western society and that of Java is the general absence in the first as compared with the pervasive presence in the second of a compelling religious mythology. This one could define as a set of national or cultural symbols commanding allegiance reasonably uniformly over a whole society, both horizontally through every region and vertically through every social class. Certainly in contemporary Western society there are no religious myths which have this kind of universal grip and relevancy. The traditional Christian myths survive largely as imposing, melancholy ruins in the flat landscape of our secular civilization. It is, of course, evident that much of our behavior is still regulated by the residues of Christian norms and values. Nevertheless, these values increasingly lack a convincing imagery of persuasive symbolism to give them urgency. If one refrains from committing adultery it is likely to be because one feels it "wouldn't be fair," or because one is too lazy, busy, or timid, rather than because Paris suffered bitterly for his rape of Helen or because Moses brought down his graven tablets from Mount Sinai. Our morality grows steadily more pragmatic— without poetry or metaphysics.

In Java, for historical reasons which are too complicated to enter into here, there is still an almost universally accepted religious mythology which commands deep emotional and intellectual adherence. This is what I shall call, for convenience, the *wayang* tradition, from the much loved shadow-play of that name which is the main preserver and transmitter of that tradition. *Wayang*, like any other metaphysical and ethical "system," is concerned to explain the universe. Though partially based on the Indian epics Mahabharata and Ramayana, the Javanese *wayang* mythology is yet an attempt to explore poetically the existential position of Javanese man, his relationships to the natural and supernatural order, to his fellow-men—and to himself. In contrast to the great religions of the Near East, however, the religion of *wayang* has no prophet, no message, no Bible, and no Redeemer. It does not conceive the world as moving in any linear trajectory, nor does it preach a universal message of salvation. It does not offer the ecstasies of the Christian apocalypse, merely the inexorable flux. The world-view expressed in this religious tradition has been aptly epitomized by Mrs. Claire Holt as "a stable world based on conflict." Yet the sense of underlying instability is no less important than the sense of permanence. If a wheel spins eternally on a fixed axis, is it changing or unchanged?

## IV

The endless variety and sharp individuality of its *dramatis personae* indicates that *wayang* reflects the variegation of human life as it is felt by the Javanese. Nevertheless, this teeming multiplicity is ordered by clearly marked dichotomies. There is, for example, the fundamental cleavage between Left and Right, *Sepuh* and *Nèm* (Old and Young), Kuråwå and Pendåwå, which at bottom grows out of a sense of the obvious dualities of the Universe: male and female, sun and earth, mountain and sea, night and day, age and youth. All are necessary and complementary to one another. Day is not day without night, and youth is not youth without age peering over its shoulder. The harmonious tension and energetic stability of this *weltanschauung* are in essential opposition to the cosmologies of Christianity and Islam in which the Supreme Being is quite unambiguous, representing only one set of "poles" (maleness, goodness, light, and reason). It must be acknowledged that recently, under Christian, European influences, probably dating back to the end of the last century, there has been a tendency in Java to simplify the older, complicated interrelationships. Tolerance of ambiguity has begun to decline, and *wayang* has tended to be devalued towards a commonplace morality play between Good and Evil.[1] The growing popularity of this type of interpretation reflects an attempt to assimilate Javanese to Western civilization. But it should always be stressed that this is not the older, subtler Javanese tradition and not the relativistic religious conception which has suffused Javanese life, religion, and art for hundreds of years. The division on the *kelir* (*wayang* screen) between Kuråwå and Pendåwå is often today taken to represent the conflict between Evil and Good. Yet the deeper complementarities and ambiguous interconnections of human existence are cunningly exposed by the irony that Left and Right are not absolute. Depending whether, at a *wayang* performance, one watches the puppets or their shadows, right becomes left and left right. Both are merely in the eye of the beholder.

The other important division in the *wayang* world stems from the close relationship between Javanese religious thinking and a particular historically determined social order. "Javanism" is a world-outlook inconceivable in an egalitarian and meritocratic society. The ancient Southeast Asian conception of the God-King, by which the temporal ruler represented divine power incarnate and the king's subjects partook of this power in exact proportion to their proximity to the throne, permeates the *wayang* world. Both symbolically and in everyday practice, the Javanese social hierarchy reflected a cosmological perspective in direct contrast to that of Islam and Christianity. These religions present a stark contrast between Man and God, engaged in direct dialogue across the infinite and silent spaces which so terrified Pascal. For the Javanese, however, the cosmos is not only teeming with life and living energy but is also elaborately ranked and ordered. Java has never had a caste system. Yet something of the pure idea of caste, shorn of its rigid Indian barbarities and with greater emphasis upon function than on birth, struck and

---

[1] This kind of interpretation has unluckily been encouraged by transient foreign commentators, who have too often imposed their own moral conceptions on a tradition they failed fully to comprehend.

maintained strong roots as the appropriate symbolic expression of an hierarchical community.[2]

Implicit in an unequal hierarchical social order is the idea that each rank or level has its own peculiar functions within the social structure. Each order is dependent on all the others. If one fails to function, all the others suffer the consequences. Thus, the King communicates with the supernatural powers and secures their benevolence; the *brahmånå* perform the rituals of state and transmit the culture of the community to the next generation; the *satryå* have the duty of administering the government and protecting the state from external attack; the traders maintain economic prosperity, while the artisans construct the material apparatus of the civilization. Out of the concept of function there now emerges the idea of morality. Precisely because all functions are interrelated, and because each order is essential to all the others, social approval for individuals within each order depends on how adequately they fulfill their order's functions. Thus, a *satryå* who behaves perfectly in the artisan "manner" is a bad *satryå*, regardless of the good work that he may in fact do. A trader who lives as a trader is a better member of society than the trader who leads the life of an ascetic *brahmånå*.[3] So there develops a stratification of moralities according to caste and class, each of which may be in contrast or conflict with the others. The harshnesses of this conception are mitigated by Buddhist influences, which prevent any absolute value being attached to a particular class or its morality. The final goal is not earthly morality but absorption into the Infinite. The ideal mode of behavior is to acquit oneself appropriately according to the "rank" to which one's *nasib* (fate) has assigned one, without attaching any permanent importance to it.

This moral pluralism suffuses the whole world of *wayang*. For example, the criticism leveled at the Kuråwå is not that they are bad men but bad *satryå*. The hero Adipati Karnå fights on the Kuråwå side but is approved of because he lives and dies as a real *satryå* should. In one early *lakon*, or play, when Karnå's high *satryå* origins are still unknown, he enters and is about to win an archery contest when he is stopped and roundly abused by the Pendåwå. They sneer at him for abandoning the appropriate life-style he inherited from his supposed father, a charioteer. The Javanese audience watching the *lakon* will undoubtedly feel disturbed at this point. But they will be upset not on the general grounds that such arrogant abuse is, humanly speaking, reprehensible, whoever the target, but because they know that all the time Karnå is really a *satryå*. Thus the Pendåwå's behavior is inappropriate, or, as the Javanese put it, *ora pantès*.

In this idea of "appropriateness" we discover a concept central to Javanese ethical theory. And this idea is itself rooted in the inter-dependencies of a complex and sophisticated hierarchical civilization. Thus although the ethical requirements of each life-style in the *wayang* may be rigid and austere, the existence of a plurality of such life-styles, each with its own code of behavior, gives the *wayang* world a wide variety of psychological contrasts, a sumptuous array of characters, and, on occasion, an unmatched moral poignancy.

---

[2] This hierarchical feeling is fundamental to the unique structure of the Javanese language, which employs two radically different basic vocabularies—called *kråmå* and *ngoko*—according to whether the person addressed is higher or lower on the social ladder than the speaker.

[3] Such is the general rule. Of course individuals with exceptional talents or magical powers may transcend these social norms. But these individuals, insofar as they successfully reveal their powers, are taken by society to be "really" members of the group to which they aspire behind the surface appearance of, say, simple traders.

In one well-known *lakon*, the young, handsome, and virtuous Salyå discovers that his bride, Déwi Satyåwati, is the daughter of a *rasekså*[4] (monstrous giant) hermit known as Begawan Bagaspati. The young couple are deeply in love. Satyåwati and her widowed father are strongly attached to one another. Salyå himself has, personally, nothing but respect for his father-in-law. Nevertheless, it is felt to be "inappropriate" for Salyå, a prominent *satryå*, to have a *rasekså* in his family. It is understood by all parties that Salyå and Satyåwati's marriage cannot be fulfilled so long as Bagaspati remains alive. Thereupon, Bagaspati orders Salyå to kill him, since he himself wishes the marriage to endure for his child's sake. And as a marriage-gift he bestows on the young man the celebrated and invincible magical weapon Tjåndåbiråwå. Salyå agrees to carry out the old *rasekså*'s wishes, though he is well aware that this murder is in its own way a violation of the *satryå* code and that he will eventually have to pay the price with his own life. The deed is done, and Salyå rides off with Satyåwati to his family's palace in Mandråkå.

Fig. 1 Salyå

---

[4] The *rasekså* are the traditional enemies of the *satryå* in most *wayang* stories. They are often taken to represent the demonic forces, where the *satryå* represent the powers of reason and order.

Fig. 2 Satyåwati

For the Javanese audience, the moral ambiguities of this simple episode are a matter of endless debate. What was Salyå's real duty? Where should Satyåwati's loyalty have lain? What were Bagaspati's real designs? Which of the three showed the deepest nobility of character? Was it Salyå, who agreed to murder to keep the honor of his *satryå* family undefiled and accepted his own violent end as a just retribution? Was it Satyåwati, who sacrificed her father for her beloved husband? Or was it Bagaspati, who put his daughter and her lover before himself yet, as he lay dying, prophesied that he would return to wreak vengeance on both?

Or another well-known example. At the height of the Last War between the Kuråwå and the Pendåwå, known as the Bråtåjudå Djåjåbinangun, Ardjunå (see Fig. 7, page 25), the best-loved of the Pendåwå, is about to engage in single combat with his elder half-brother Adipati Karnå (see Fig. 10, page 28). In great anxiety of mind, he turns to his spiritual mentor, Prabu Kresnå (see Fig. 8, page 26), and confides his deep unwillingness to fight. The Kuråwå, in spite of everything, are his brothers and cousins, and in such a fratricidal slaughter the victors will be more wretched than the vanquished. At least the latter will attain the real goal of every *satryå*, an honorable death on the field of battle. Kresnå answers briefly that the true *satryå* is never swayed from the path of duty by personal sentiment or family feeling. In any case, it has long since been fated that Ardjunå shall destroy his brother Karnå. Karnå himself knows that he is destined to die at Ardjunå's hands; yet he does not flinch from the struggle. As a real *satryå*, Ardjunå must pursue his destiny without complaint or useless lamentation.

Again the morality of the traditional ruling class is displayed in its most austere form. Feelings of family solidarity and piety, which might be indulged with propriety by members of another social group, are forbidden to the *satryå*. In such a world, one can only judge a man's moral worth when one knows who he is.

This sense of loyalty to a caste code should not, however, be seen in isolation, as merely the selfish vanity and empty posturing of a privileged group. In the mysterious and sacred *lakon, Semar Påpå*, the Pendåwå kingdom of Ngamartå is

Fig. 3 Bagaspati

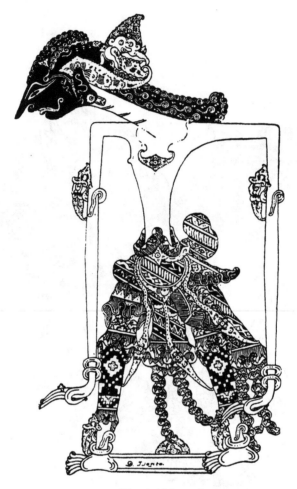

Fig. 4 Abimanju

struck by an inexplicable plague. A seer warns that the pestilence can only be dispelled by the death of Semar (see Fig. 17, page 37), the loyal servant of the Pendåwå who has waited on them from birth and rescued them from countless difficulties. Deeply troubled, Prabu Judistirå (see Fig. 5, page 23), eldest of the Pendåwå, calls his brothers into council. After long debate, they decide that the state and community, which they as *satryå* are pledged to defend, must take precedence even over the life of their beloved retainer. Accordingly, Judistirå orders his nephew, the young prince Abimanju, Ardjunå's eldest son, to lead the old man into the neighboring forest and there put him to death. But when Abimanju and Semar are alone together, the tender-hearted young prince cannot bring himself to carry out his uncle's command. He releases Semar and hurries away.

Sentiment has begun to change in Java today. But traditionally Abimanju's behavior was regarded as a lapse from real *satryå* morality. The young man acts like a woman or a child, not as a *satryå*.. The really moral men are Semar, who, as a retainer, agrees to die for his master, and Judistirå, who, though devoted to Semar, sacrifices his personal feelings for the welfare of his subjects.

## V

Having now considered the deep Javanese recognition of the logical and social necessity of a moral pluralism, along "caste" lines, some attention should perhaps be given to structural variations within these "castes." For the characters of *wayang* are not simply divided into Left and Right, Kuråwå and Pendåwå, gods, kings, *brahmånå, satryå,* princesses, giants, apes, and clowns, each with their own style and way of life. Each of these general categories contains within itself a wide range of personalities, which must be analyzed, however summarily, in their aspect as human types and as bearers of contrasting values.

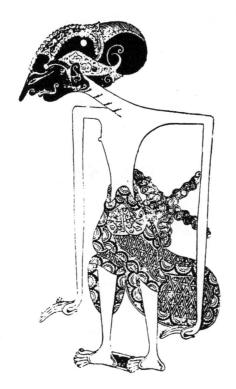

Fig. 5 Judistirå

### *Judistirå*

The eldest of the five Pendåwå is Prabu Judistirå. He is the pure type of the Good King. The blood in his veins is white. He never raises his voice in anger, never fights, and never rejects a request from anyone, however humble. His time is spent in meditation and the accumulation of wisdom. Unlike the other heroes, whose chief magical attributes are weapons, Judistirå's sacred heirloom is the mysterious Kalimåsådå, a holy text containing the secrets of religion and the universe. He is, above all, the disinterested intellectual, ruling his kingdom with perfect justice and aloof benevolence. In the complete lack of ostentatious ornament, the gentle, introspective inclination of the head, and the aristocratic refinement of feature, one recognizes the ideal portrait of the passionless *Panditå Ratu* (Priest-King).

Fig. 6 Wrekudårå

### Wrekudårå (Bimå)

Wrekudårå is the most feared of warriors, creating havoc with his terrible club and atrocious fingernails (the Påntjånåkå). He disdains to ride in a chariot and strides through forests and deserts and over mountains and seas without any difficulty. He scorns pomp and finery. He bows to no one. Even to the gods he speaks in *ngoko*, the form of Javanese used to social inferiors. Merciless to his enemies, gigantic, ungainly, heavily muscled, hairy, with protruding eyes and thunderous voice, he is the complete contrast to his elder brother. Nevertheless, his unswerving honesty, loyalty, fortitude, and military skill make him among the most admired figures in *wayang*.

## *Ardjunå*

What is one to say of Ardjunå? Unequaled warrior on the battlefield, yet physically delicate and beautiful as a girl, tender-hearted yet iron-willed, a hero whose wives and mistresses are legion yet who is capable of the most extreme discipline and self-denial, a *satryå* with a deep feeling for family loyalty who yet forces himself to kill his own half-brother, he is, to the older generation of Javanese, the epitome of the whole man. In contrast to Judistirå, he is joyfully at home in the world. His amorous adventures never cease to delight the Javanese, yet in a strange way he is in complete contrast to Don Juan. So great is his physical beauty and refinement, that princesses and maid-servants alike hurry to offer themselves to him. It is they who are honored, not Ardjunå. And in contrast to Wrekudårå he represents the physical grace and gentleness of heart which generations of Javanese have so highly prized.

Fig. 7 Ardjunå

## *Kresnå*

Kresnå and his brother Bålådéwå are first cousins to the Pendåwå. Kresnå is part God, an incarnation of the mighty Wisnu. He is the consummate politician, diplomat, and strategist of war. By far the most intellectually brilliant of the Pendåwå faction, it is Kresnå who makes their final victory possible. On the other hand, he is a conscienceless liar and an unscrupulous schemer who never hesitates to break the rules when he feels it necessary. Though a *satryå*, he repeatedly ignores the lesser values of the *satryå* class. Only the duty to carry out the will of the gods and his own destiny claim his allegiance. He is cynical where Judistirå is pious, humorous and

Fig. 8 Kresnå

sarcastic where Wrekudårå is savage, stern and inflexible where Ardjunå shows human weakness. In the long struggle between Kuråwå and Pendåwå, both sides use treachery and cunning. Only Kresnå, however, wins approval, since his ultimate aims accord with the will of the gods to destroy the Kuråwå and since he himself is of divine origin. These factors make his actions appropriate.

Fig. 9 Bålådéwå

### Bålådéwå

Kresnå's brother, Prabu Bålådéwå, King of Mandurå, sides with the Kuråwå, yet in his own way is no less striking and admirable a figure. Given to sudden generous enthusiasms, unstinting in his loyalties, brave, hot-tempered, direct, and undoubtedly stupid, he is in marked contrast to Kresnå, who, indeed, consistently manipulates and outmaneuvers him. Yet at the end of the Last War, when all the heroes, including Kresnå himself, are dead and gone, it is Bålådéwå who is left alone to guard and bring up Parikesit, Ardjunå's infant grandson, who will become the ancestor of the Kings of Java.

Fig. 10 Karnå

## Karnå

Though in every respect Ardjunå's equal in physical perfection, military skill, and moral sensitivity, he dies at Ardjunå's hands because the Gods have willed it so. When still a new-born baby he was abandoned by his mother, Déwi Kunti Nalibråtå (see Fig. 51, page 77), who was later also to give birth to the Pendåwå. A simple charioteer brought him up. Eventually, the Kuråwå, looking for a champion against the Pendåwå, took him into service, raised him up, and honored him, finally making him Adipati (Viceroy) in Ngawånggå. The Pendåwå, on the other hand, while respecting his prowess, sneered at his low origins and rejected his company. Later, when it became known that he was really Judistirå's elder brother, the *satryå* sense of honor told him that ingratitude to the Kuråwå King would be more disgraceful than fighting against his own family. Though he clearly recognizes that King Sujudånå, his master, has repeatedly violated the *satryå* code, he will not abandon him.[5]

The Javanese attitude to Karnå was brought home to me once very vividly when I was speaking with an elderly Javanese official about a friend of his who had fought on the side of the Dutch during the Revolution. The friend had been embittered when some of his family were murdered by a gang of nationalist youths in the anarchic days after the Proclamation of Independence. He had also been well treated by the Dutch. The elderly Javanese was an ardent patriot, yet as he spoke of his former school-friend he slipped easily and almost unconsciously into a comparison with Adipati Karnå. His friend, too, had fought on the wrong side, but for reasons which seemed to him sufficient. And he had fought with courage and honor. One could not call him a *pengchianat* (traitor) like those who had "crossed over" from faintheartedness, lack of principle, or hope of gain. He did not know if his friend was still alive. He had never seen him since and, in a sense, did not wish to. Yet he fully accepted and respected what he had done.

---

[5] Compare, for example, stanzas 5 and 6 of the beautiful poem *Tripama* by G. P. A. A. Mangkunegara IV, in his *Dwidja Isjwara* (Albert Rusche & Co., Soerakarta, 1899), pp. 102–104:

| | |
|---|---|
| Wonten malih kinarjå palupi | There is one other (hero) who should be held as an example, |
| Surjåputrå narpati Ngawånggå | The son of Suryå, ruler of Ngawånggå, |
| Lan Pandåwå tur kadangé | Although the Pendåwå's own brother, |
| Lèn jajah tunggil ibu | (With different father, yet the same mother) |
| Suwitå mring Sri Kurupati | He served the Lord Kurupati |
| Anèng nagri Ngastinå | In the city of Ngastinå |
| Kinarjå gul-agul | And became his champion. |
| Manggålå golongan ing prang | Commander of armies, |
| Bråtåjudå ingadegken Sénåpati | In the Bråtåjudå War he was made battle-chief |
| Ngalågå ing Koråwå | Over all the Koråwå. |
| Dèn mungsuhken kadangé pribadi | Sent out against his own brother |
| Aprang tanding lan Sang Danandjåjå | He fought in single combat with Lord Danandjåjå (Ardjunå) |
| Sri Karnå sukå manahé | Yet the Lord Karnå's heart was glad |
| Dé gonirå pikantuk | Because he had found a way |
| Margå dènjå arså males sih- | To requite the love |
| Irå Sang Durjudånå | Of King Durjudånå (Sujudånå). |
| Marmantå kalangkung | Therefore he now exerted to the utmost |
| Dènjå ngetog kasudiran | All his soldier's skill and courage. |
| Aprang ramé Karnå mati djinemparing | In the heat of battle Karnå died, struck by an arrow, |
| Sumbågå wirå tåmå | Renowned, a matchless warrior. |

*Kumbåkarnå*

Similar to Karnå in his outlook and morality, Radèn Kumbåkarnå, hero of the Ramayana, also dies to defend a king whom he realizes has dishonored his position. He knows that he is going to die, shorn limb from limb. Yet, unlike his younger brother, Radèn Wibisånå (see Fig. 55, page 90), who "crosses over" to side with Råmå and Justice, he refuses to desert his elder brother, Prabu Dåsåmukå (Rahwånå) (see Fig. 54, page 89), in his hour of need. The main difference between Karnå and

Fig. 11 Kumbåkarnå

Kumbåkarnå is one of physical type. Kumbåkarnå is the most colossal of giants and is represented by the largest *wayang* puppet of all, sometimes one and a half meters in height. To look at, he is the monstrous giant type in extreme form, with brutal red features, bulbous nose, hyperthyroid eyes, clumsy, hairy torso, and wolf-like fangs. These are all physical characteristics which the Javanese find repugnant. Yet Kumbåkarnå is among the best-loved of *wayang* figures, and the prize example of inner nobility and purity belying external appearance.[6]

The Kuråwå are an equally varied group, but two figures stand out for particular attention. These are Dahjang Durnå and Prabu Sujudånå.

## Dahjang Durnå

Durnå is a *brahmånå*, magician, and teacher. When they were all still boys, both Kuråwå and Pendåwå learnt the arts of war from him, and to the end he retains a deep affection for his favorite pupil Ardjunå, though they are arrayed on opposite sides in the Last War. The tendency in *wayang* today is to portray him as a half-sinister, half-comic figure, but this is not the older, traditional perspective. He was then Kresnå's great adversary, but with the Gods against him and without Kresnå's divinity. As a sign of his extraordinary learning and magical power, he alone of mortals wins a heavenly nymph, Déwi Wilutåmå, as his bride; by her he has a single, adored son, named Bambang Aswåtåmå (see Fig. 29, page 55).

In the long struggle between Kuråwå and Pendåwå, he matches Kresnå trick for trick, stratagem for stratagem. He too stands outside the *satryå* code, obeying the Machiavellian morality which also guides Kresnå. And in the Bråtåjudå Djåjåbinangun, when he finally takes the field, his power is still so great that the Pendåwå and their armies turn and flee. Ardjunå himself refuses to face his now aged and crippled teacher. As a last resort, Kresnå orders Wrekudårå to kill an elephant which by chance bears the same name as Durnå's son—Aswåtåmå. In

---

[6] Compare stanzas 3 and 4 of *Tripama*:

| | |
|---|---|
| Wonten malih tuladan prajogi | There is another fitting model, |
| Satrijå gung nagri ing Ngalengkå | A great *satryå* from the city of Ngalengkå. |
| Sang Kumbåkarnå arané | Lord Kumbåkarnå was his name. |
| Tur iku warnå diju | Though outwardly he was like a monstrous giant |
| Suprandéné gajuh utami | In his heart he strove for the highest excellence. |
| Duk wiwit prang Ngalengkå | When the war in Ngalengkå began |
| Dènjå darbé atur | He offered counsel |
| Mring råkå amrih rahardjå | To his brother, to keep him safe. |
| Dåsåmukå tan kéguh ing atur jekti | But it seemed that Dåsåmukå was not moved by his words |
| | |
| Déné mungsuh wanårå | Saying that the enemy were merely apes. |
| Kumbåkarnå kinon mangsah djurit | Kumbåkarnå was ordered to lead the battle fray |
| Mring kang råkå sirå tan lenggånå | By his brother Dåsåmukå, and did not refuse. |
| Nglungguhi kasatrijané | Fulfilling his duty as a *satryå* |
| Ing tékad tan asurud | Steadfast in his determination, |
| Amung tjiptå labuh nagari | His only thought was to serve his country. |
| Lan nolih jajah rénå | Recalling that his father and mother |
| Myang luluhuripun | And all his ancestors |
| Wus mukti anèng Ngalengkå | Had won glory and honor in Ngalengkå, |
| Mangké arså rinusak ing bålå kapi | Which monkey armies now threatened to destroy, |
| Punagi mati ngrånå | He vowed to die in battle. |

Fig. 12 Durnå

simulated triumph, the Pendåwå cry out, "Aswåtåmå is dead! Aswåtåmå is dead!" In a daze of grief, Durnå turns to Judistirå, whom he knows has never lied, and asks him if it is true. Ruthlessly goaded by Kresnå, Judistirå unwillingly confirms the half-truth.[7] Convinced at last, the old *brahmånå* stands silent, motionless, in the midst of battle. No one dares approach him in his agony and despair, until the impetuous Drestådjumenå rushes up and strikes off his head. All feel that a terrible and impious deed has been performed and that retribution will be exacted. Both Kuråwå and Pendåwå unite to perform the full funerary obsequies.

Fig. 13 Drestådjumenå

---

[7] The half-truth depends on the double meaning of the Javanese word *èsti*, which can mean either "indeed" or "elephant." Thus, Judistirå's famous reply can be interpreted as either "Indeed Aswåtåmå is dead" or "The elephant Aswåtåmå is dead."

### Sujudånå

Eldest of the ninety-nine Kuråwå brothers, he is King of Ngastinå, most powerful and glittering of the ancient mythological Javanese capitals. He is a great monarch, yet fated to destroy himself and his house. Though vain and easily swayed by his advisers, he is a worthy antagonist for the Pendåwå. Indeed, without him, the Pendåwå would not be the Pendåwå. The Gods have doomed Ngastinå long before he was born. As Jehovah hardened Pharaoh's heart, so Sujudånå is inevitably drawn

Fig. 14 Sujudånå

by his destiny into the fatal course which brings the Kuråwå to their ruin. On the last night of the Bråtåjudå, he alone of the Kuråwå chiefs is left. In his tent he meditates in silence on all that has come to pass. What is the use of further bloodshed? Only a handful of faithful retainers remains alive. Why not surrender? Yet, after all, he is a great *satryå* and a great king. Hundreds of thousands have loyally died for him. Now it is his turn to die for them. When dawn comes he goes forth to combat the terrible Wrekudårå. Both armies watch in silence as the two are locked in a desperate struggle. Neither can gain the upper hand. Wrekudårå is more powerful, but Sujudånå more deft and quick. For the last time, Kresnå intervenes to tip the balance. Although it is strictly against the *satryå* rules for single combat, he directs Wrekudårå to smash Sujudånå's exposed thigh. Out of desperation, Wrekudårå obeys, and Sujudånå, who has fought with high honor, sinks to the ground in agony, now to fall unresisting prey to the ferocious talons of his adversary. The *lakon* describing Sujudånå's end is to this day rarely performed in Java, so great is the aura of tragedy and disaster which surrounds it. The fall of the greatest of Javanese kingdoms and the pitiful destruction of its mighty ruler seem to presage untimely events and contemporary calamities.

The women in the *wayang* world are much less varied in their typology than the men. Yet significant contrasts do exist. One to which the Javanese are very fond of pointing is that between Ardjunå's main wives, Déwi Sumbådrå and Déwi Srikandi.

### Sumbådrå

Sumbådrå is very much the lady—elegant, gentle, reserved, utterly loyal and obedient to her husband. She represents the ideal type of the aristocratic Javanese woman.

Fig. 15 Sumbådrå

### Srikandi

Srikandi is the exact opposite of Sumbådrå. Talkative, strong-willed, warm-hearted, fond of hunting, an excellent archer, she is quite ready to debate with Ardjunå or take on a passing *satryå* in battle. She enjoys traveling about Java, either in search of her periodically missing husband or seeking adventures of her own. In the Indian original of the Mahabharata, Srikandi is really a man who has been changed into a woman. In Java, this is not the case; but perhaps the "masculine" side of her character owes something to this long-forgotten source. For the Javanese, Srikandi is the honored type of the active, energetic, disputatious, generous, go-getting woman. Between herself and Sumbådrå there is no jealousy, rather a deep, understanding affection—though one gets the impression that Srikandi is sometimes a little impatient with Sumbådrå's excessively lady-like helplessness whenever any trouble arises. Perhaps Sumbådrå in turn feels that Srikandi does not always really act like a dignified lady.

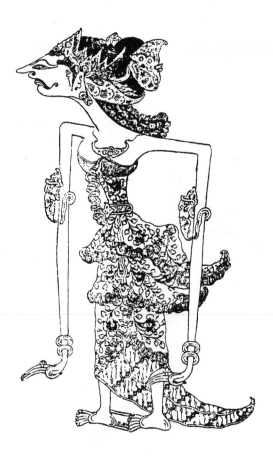

Fig. 16 Srikandi

Fig. 17 Semar

## Kjai Lurah Semar

One last figure remains to be considered. He comes from the clown (*punåkawan*) class. There is no room here to go into the important and difficult problem of the general significance of these *punåkawan* in Javanese folk-lore. Suffice it to say that Semar, most venerable of these *punåkawan*, is probably the best loved figure in all *wayang*, a favorite of young and old alike. Partly this is because Semar, though a humble and comical retainer, is yet the most powerful of Gods, so that the Lord Shiwa himself, Batårå Guru, must on occasion submit to him. Partly it is just because he is a clown, a man of the people, to whom the rules of *satryå* behavior do not apply, and who by his presence alone offers an implied criticism of the whole range of *satryå* values. Partly it is because Semar is the physical denial of the *satryå* type. He is immensely fat, with heavy breasts and a vast behind. He is ornamented like a woman, his clothes are those of a man, yet his face is that of neither man nor woman. He is the repository of the highest wisdom, yet this flashes from in between his gentle jokes, his clowning, and even his persistent, uncontrollable farting. Anyone who has witnessed a Javanese shadow-play will recall the wave of deep affection and respect which flows out of the audience towards Semar when he appears. It is said that one of the most distinguished professors at the University of Indonesia in Djakarta owed his unique following among the Javanese students less to his high academic attainments than to his physical resemblance to Semar and his reputation for a special combination of wisdom and comicality.

Fig. 18 Guru

## VI

The universal affection and knowledge of this *wayang* mythology at all levels and in all areas of Java means that little village children from their earliest years are acquainted with the characters discussed above, not merely their names but their physical, psychological, and ethical traits. And their acquaintance is not abstract but strongly visual, since *wayang* performances are frequent and most villages have sets of rough wooden or cardboard *wayangs* with which the children can play and practice by themselves.

More important still, in the traditional view, all the main characters, except perhaps Durnå, are held in high honor. No hierarchy is imposed. Kresnå is not "better" than Ardjunå, nor Wrekudårå than Judistirå. Each is a totally accepted part of the *wayang* world, which in turn is regarded as a model for Javanese life, lived on a high plane of moral intensity. To a limited degree, of course, popularity does vary by area and class. The proverbially hot-headed, impetuous Madurese are known to have a special fondness for Bålådéwå, whose kingdom, Mandurå, is generally supposed to be the same as Madura. The subtle Solonese may find Kresnå more appealing than his brother. In the same way, the villager may identify more closely with Semar and his sons than with Judistirå and Karnå, while the children of a prince may be educated to look at Ardjunå as their prime model. But even here the differences are not great. The idea of the *satryå* is only to a limited degree associated with a closed class. Its class content has progressively given way to a more general ethical content to which even villagers may aspire. All these variations according to region and social class are minor. Madurese and Solonese, high officials and peasants alike share a deep love and respect for the whole gamut of *wayang* and its chief protagonists.

The importance of this is that it was traditionally from the ethical and religious aspects of *wayang* that the education of Javanese children drew its inspiration. The heroes of *wayang* were the consciously approved models by which a child grew up. Whereas Christian religious education arises from general abstract precepts of universal application, a *wayang* education develops out of a set of concrete mythological models and examples. The Javanese child learns from the models and examples of behavior the philosophical teachings which will later orient him to the outside world. And it is not merely the moral sense of the Javanese child which is molded by *wayang* but also his aesthetic awareness. This is partly because in traditional Javanese, as in ancient Greek, civilization there is no clear line separating the idea of the good and the beautiful. The same word (*saé*) is used for both. Both, in a sense, are merely aspects of the appropriate or harmonious, which, as I have suggested before, lies at the deepest roots of Javanese culture. Accordingly, what is good is beautiful, and what is beautiful is good. The cultivation of the aesthetic aspect of a child's sensibility is a key aspect of Javanese education. This is not, as in Western society, to provide a chance for gifted children to develop their talents but in order that every child should learn to order all aspects of his life in a harmonious way. Even in modern Javanese schools, this older idea is still maintained. In the *Taman Siswå* school system, founded in 1922 and guided until his death by Ki Hadjar Dewantoro, every effort is made to avoid a division and separation between the technical-scientific, moral, and aesthetic aspects of education. Dancing, particularly, is taught, not for social reasons, or to provide opportunities for young people to meet one another, but to develop physical grace, a sense of rhythm, and a harmonious personality.

## VII

It is not, however, simply that the abstract principles of the Near Eastern religions, and the rationalism which has succeeded them in Western society, are applicable, by implication, to all men regardless of social position and social function. We do of course, in theory, expect the same morality from the business executive and his janitor. But they are also universal regardless of personality structure, psychological bent, and physical type. We are not in the least inclined to adapt our standards of moral excellence according to the personality and station of the individual to be judged. This is, of course, not simply a question of the Christian tradition. It is also a consequence of the destruction of feudal society and the rise of modern capitalism and secular individualism. The assumptions of a competitive and egalitarian society are basically that a gigantic race is being run, in which all should have an equal opportunity to take part, and with unified, well-understood criteria for success. Whatever its advantages, this conception of society inevitably narrows the range of personality types which will win unqualified general acceptance and approval. After all, a race in which camels, tortoises, apes, and iguanas compete with one another is likely to be confused and confusing. The trend is naturally to fit course and prize to the camels and let the devil take the hindmost.

The characteristic patterns of traditional Javanese society present a striking contrast. Precisely because the moral and physical models are enshrined in a universally accepted mythology, that of *wayang*, the young Javanese is presented with a wide choice of models for his own personality, which he can be sure will win approval anywhere in Javanese society. Where there is no race, the animals can live together in harmony. Since Ardjunå, Wrekudårå, and Judistirå are all held in honor, both the heavily built, active, but inarticulate boy and the delicately boned, introspective child have acceptable ways in which their personalities and physical traits can evolve without unnecessary spiritual violence being done to them. Ardjunå's great sexual magnetism provides assurance to the small and frail child that he will not suffer in everyday socio-sexual competition. The child with a talent for oratory and politics has his Kresnå, the boy with a taste for intellectual activities and meditation his Judistirå, the hot-tempered, courageous youngster his Bålådéwå. Triumph over low social origin and snobbery is typified by Karnå. Between Wibisånå and Kumbåkarnå a young man has models both for unquestioning loyalty to the political community (in our era, "my country, right or wrong") or for abstract love of principle (a supranational attachment, perhaps, to humanism, Islam, or Communism). For women the same applies. The young Javanese girl can aspire to Sumbådrå's gentle, languishing charm, or, should she look for a more active and vigorous role, the energetic warmth of Srikandi. One might note in passing that not only have the women's units in the Indonesian National Army taken Srikandi as their model, but also the first woman guerrilla who landed in West Irian during the 1962 liberation campaign was widely referred to as "our Srikandi," both by President Sukarno and by the general public.

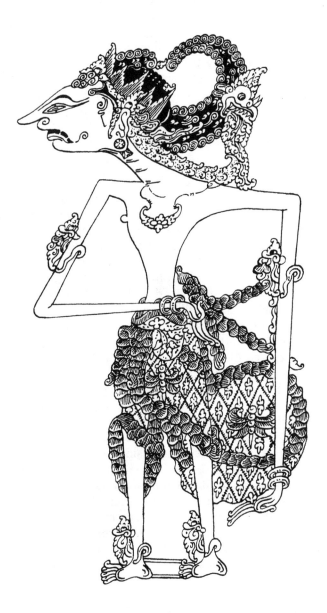

Fig. 19 Såmbå

The models, of course, are not all admirable. *Wayang* is too rich in types and too close to Javanese life for that. The reprehensible models, however, by their very concrete visibility, provide an effective foil for the admirable examples. People in Java will often refer to a good-looking, but weak and idle, young man as a "Såmbå," since Såmbå, Kresnå's son, is just such a person. There are other figures, such as Sangkuni (see Fig. 32, page 58) or Durasåsånå (see Fig. 33, page 59) in the *satryå* class, Pétruk (see Fig. 40, page 66) and Togog (see Fig. 38, page 64) in the clown class, who may be referred to in the same way as specific, typical personifications of certain types of inappropriate or strongly disapproved behavior.

In brief, then, it seems reasonable to suggest that the universal hold which *wayang* has over the Javanese population at all levels, and the rich variety of concrete models it offers, afford a real legitimation for widely contrasting social and psychological types. In other words, tolerance is taught, and later maintained, by a mythology which informs and suffuses the whole Javanese tradition. It is not by any means necessarily an innate characteristic of the Javanese people as such. Rather, it is structurally related to both a static and traditional social order and the pervasiveness of *wayang* as a source of religion, morality, and philosophy.

## VIII

For those who find much that is admirable, gentle, and humane in this tolerance, the recognition of its historical and sociological basis necessarily arouses anxieties for its survival in the present age. The rapid decline of the traditional order since Independence has clearly threatened the older moral pluralism. The rise of a new pseudo-traditional elite in Djakarta, the spread of commercial urbanism, and the emergence of nationalism as the single dominant standard by which ever more aspects of a person's life are being assessed and judged, all are undoubtedly, if slowly, undermining the older, structurally conditioned tolerance.

*Wayang* itself seems, in the more metropolitan centers, to be changing rapidly from an education to a mere entertainment. In many different ways, the influence of nationalism and Western civilization are becoming more and more obtrusive. Among the symptoms which point in this direction are:

i) A growing trend to perceive in *wayang* a simple conflict between Good and Evil, with a resulting impoverishment of its aesthetic and moral complexity. The political parties have accelerated this trend by their attempts to exploit *wayang* for propaganda purposes. "We" become the Pendåwå, "they" the Kuråwå—with obvious consequences in terms of crudeness and simplification.

ii) The reduction of *wayang*'s elaborate formal structure into a series of battle-scenes linked by banal jokes and sentimental boudoir interludes. Here the influence of the cinema is unmistakable, since fighting, comedy, and sentiment are the essentials of most films that Indonesians see. The current pressure to shorten a *wayang* performance from a whole night to two or three hours reflects again the assimilation of *wayang* to modern commercial entertainment.

iii) Increasing criticism of the traditional "philosophizing" of the puppeteer (*dalang*) as "feudal" and "out of date." There is a growing demand for the *dalang* to be "modern." This modernity, however, turns out to be simply the more superficial *idées reçues* of Westernized bourgeois culture. There are three areas where this embourgeoisement of *wayang* is clearest. a) The reinterpretation of most sexual relationships (e.g., Ardjunå's with Sumbådrå) in terms of bourgeois "romance," often with remarkably Victorian overtones. b) The "rationalizing" of marvelous or supernatural elements in the *wayang* stories along scientific or pseudo-scientific lines, in much the same spirit as nineteenth century Western "criticism" of Biblical miracles. c) A pious moralizing of unacceptable non-bourgeois characteristics in *wayang*. This is most frequently expressed in the search for symbolic interpretations of *wayang*. (For example, the Pendåwå are taken to be symbols of parts of the human body.) This allows inconvenient aspects of the Pendåwå's several characters to be explained away as "metaphors." The same tendency is at work in elaborate justifications of apparently "bad" actions on the part of the "good" faction, which have no real basis in the *wayang* stories themselves.

iv) Ironically, the one element of traditional *wayang* which was always explicitly contemporary has been progressively abstracted from everyday life. By age-old custom, the humor of the *punåkawan* was deliberately anachronistic, often taking the form of sharp ridicule of contemporary abuses and shrewd criticism of contemporary political and economic conditions. Recently, however, this form of contemporaneity has been increasingly inhibited and even harassed by provincial officialdom, which is finding criticism, especially from below, increasingly hard to put up with.[8] This has forced the *punåkawan* to turn to a generalized, farcical, or fantastic form of humor.

v) The ascendancy within the *wayang* constellations of certain "models" over others. Here the figures of Ardjunå and Judistirå are significant omens. It is already apparent, for example, that the younger generation of Javanese are tending to concentrate their main affection less on these two heroes than on Kresnå, Wrekudårå, and Wrekudårå's son, Gatutkåtjå (see Fig. 20, p. 44)—a smaller and more physically attractive version of his father, notable for his unhesitating, uncritical loyalty and patriotism—whom President Sukarno has explicitly said should be the model for the new Indonesian Man. Judistirå's aloof meditativeness and gentle search for justice are less and less held in esteem. Ardjunå's sexual prowess is no longer seen simply as a necessary attribute of the complete *satryå* but is either frowned on by Islamic and Western-influenced puritanism or sniggered at by the new metropolitan sophisticates. On the other hand, the cinema, by the "he-man" heroes that it tends to popularize, has helped to upset the previous relationship between the figures, say, of Ardjunå and Wrekudårå. Whereas traditionally these two represented contrasting but equally impressive types of virility, nowadays one tends to find Ardjunå criticized by younger Javanese as effeminate—surely something inconceivable as little as thirty years ago.

In the political sphere, two instructive trends are particularly evident. The diplomacy and cunning of Kresnå, which in traditional *wayang* were a function of his celestial origins and his high overriding purpose to execute the will of the Gods, have tended to become detached from both and to be transformed into a justification for a rootless, ruthless Machiavellism and a delight in intrigue and political chicane for its own sake. The older balance between Kumbåkarnå and Wibisånå has also gradually been upset. Whereas an older generation found both heroes admirable but Wibisånå the more noble since he chose humanity and justice over family loyalty and gratitude, many Javanese today feel uneasy about the contrast. The spread of nationalism has made Wibisånå's abandonment of his native land for the cause of "humanism" and a supranational standard of justice, ambiguous and even suspect. Kumbakårnå's outlook, generally rather speciously characterized as "my country right or wrong," fits more easily with present sentiment; and, as a result, the prestige of this amiable giant now stands higher than his younger brother's.

---

[8] For example, late in 1963 the popular Garèng of the celebrated Sriwedari *wayang wong* troupe was arrested by the police in Solo on the grounds that he had made jokes critical of the government. The man was eventually released with a warning.

Fig. 20 Gatutkåtjå

These are, as it were, signs of the times, largely visible in the big cities of Java, where the traditional hierarchical order has disintegrated fastest. In the villages change takes place far more slowly, and it is there that the old Javanese culture undoubtedly maintains its most stubborn hold. Nevertheless, autumn is in the air. On the tree of Javanese culture the leaves are dropping one by one. The question now is whether the roots will nourish fresh leaves and flowers for a new spring-time. Will the tradition survive the extinction of its social basis? Can *wayang* be sustained and renewed from within? Can new institutional and structural supports be developed for Javanese tolerance as the older generations knew it?

It is not simply out of nostalgia that an attempt has been made here to discuss the problem of Javanese tolerance. It is out of an instinctive conviction that tolerance in all human communities is a highly fragile thing, especially a tolerance which is not simply an ignoring of nonconformities that do not threaten us or impinge directly on our lives, but which springs from a genuine respect for human variety and human personality as such. Doubtless there was much to dislike and condemn in the old Javanese cultural tradition. Yet, partly by historical accident but partly also, I believe, out of a deep awareness of the complex inter-relatedness of human existence, traditional Javanese civilization developed a style of ethics, morality, and philosophy, best expressed in *wayang*, which helped to give each man a sense of his own dignity and honor and sustained and legitimized a tolerance which one cannot but profoundly respect.

# Appendix I
# Supplementary Characters

*Betari Durgå* is the goddess of violence, darkness, and death. Her abode is in Sétrågåndåmaju, where she holds sway over ghosts, vampires, and other malevolent spirits. In the *lakons* she is always associated with the Left (Kuråwå) faction and unceasingly schemes to destroy the Pendåwå. Most dreaded of the Gods, even her husband, Batårå Guru, cannot prevail against her will. It is only Semar before whom she flees in helpless terror.

Fig. 21 Durgå

Fig. 22 Narådå

*Batårå Narådå* is an elder brother of Batårå Guru and his chief adviser and emissary. As in the case of Semar, a grotesque shape is associated with great supernatural power. Like Semar, too, he conceals his great wisdom and subtlety behind a squeaky voice and a wry, comic manner. Narådå carries out Batårå Guru's orders but generally contrives to interpret them in favor of the Pendåwå.

*Batårå Suryå* is the Sun-God, source and giver of life. When the Pendåwå's mother, Déwi Kunti, was still an unmarried virgin, she was seduced by Suryå and eventually gave birth to the infant Karnå. The mother soon abandoned her child, but Suryå always loved and watched over his son. He shares Karnå's ambiguous position in the *lakons*. When Kresnå, enraged by Kuråwå treachery during the final negotiations before the outbreak of the Bråtåjudå, assumes his World-Destroyer manifestation and threatens to annihilate Ngastinå out of hand, it is Suryå who descends, soothes him, and persuades him to resume his human shape. Since Karnå fights for the Kuråwå, Suryå is usually associated with the Left too.

Fig. 23 Suryå

Fig. 24 Baju

*Sang Hyang Baju* is a son of Batårå Guru and God of the Winds. He is the father of two of the most powerful protagonists of the *lakons*, Radèn Wrekudårå and the White Ape, Hanoman. As an outward sign of their family relationship these three figures are the only ones in *wayang* to have the terrible razor-sharp fingernails (Påntjånåkå) and to wear the magical *polèng* loin-cloth, whose red, white, black, and yellow checks symbolize the four super-deities Bråmå, Guru (Shiwa), Wisnu, and Suryå. As Wrekudårå's father, Baju is usually reckoned on the side of the Pendåwå.

*Prabu Matswåpati*, the aged king of Wiråtå, acts as the Pendåwå's mentor and protector. Though his sister, Déwi Durgandini, was the common great-grandmother of the Kuråwå and Pendåwå, he gives his daughter, Déwi Utari, in marriage to Radèn Abimanju, Ardjunå's son (and his own great-great-great-nephew!).
From this union Parikesit is born, ancestor of the historical kings of Java. It is at the court of Wiråtå that the Pendåwå take refuge when their fortunes are lowest. Matswåpati himself helps them build the glittering palace of Ngamartå. And ultimately all three of his sons—Sétå, Utårå, and Wratsångkå—fight and die for the Pendåwå in the Last War.

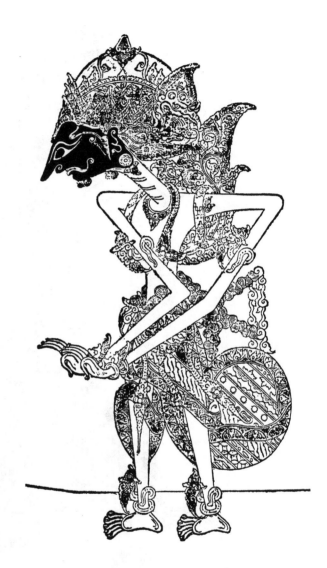

Fig. 25 Matswåpati

Fig. 26 Abjåså

*Begawan Abjåså* is the common grandfather of the Kuråwå and the Pendåwå. He was once King of Ngastinå but in middle age abandoned his court to devote himself to religious meditation and ascesis. During the Bråtåjudå he reappears to advise and console the Pendåwå. When the war has been brought to its bloody close, it is Abjåså who personally performs the solemn rituals of purification.

Fig. 27 Bhismå

*Resi Bhismå*, being Ngastinå's elder statesman, is loved and respected by Kuråwå and Pendåwå alike. Though strongly opposed to Sujudånå's policies, he sides with the Left faction and leads the Kuråwå armies at the opening of the Bråtåjudå, killing all three of Matswåpati's sons with his own hands. As a young man he had sworn to remain *wadat* (celibate) all his life. When Déwi Ambalikå wished to marry him, he jokingly threatened her with his bow and arrow. Accidentally his finger slipped and the arrow sped to her heart. Her ghost swore vengeance, and in the Last War Bhismå dies at the hands of Srikandi, Ardjunå's warrior-wife, in whom Ambalikå has been reincarnated.

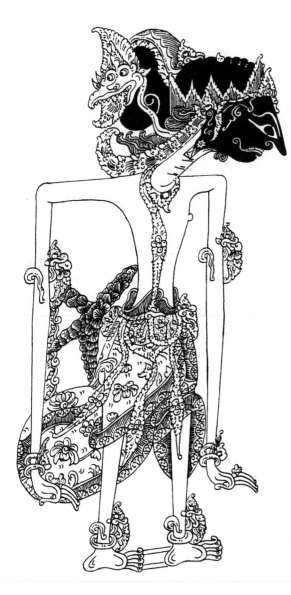

*Prabu Drupådå* is King of Tjempålåredjå and a close ally of the Pendåwå. His two daughters, Drupadi and Srikandi are respectively married to Judistirå and Ardjunå. An old enmity exists between Drupådå and Dahjang Durnå. It is thanks to Drupådå that the old *brahmånå* is crippled and deformed. The vendetta works itself out in the Bråtåjudå when Drupådå's son, Drestådjumenå, kills Durnå, and Durnå's son, Aswåtåmå, retaliates after the war is over by murdering Drestådjumenå, Srikandi, and Drupådå's grandson, Påntjåwålå, in their sleep.

Fig. 28 Drupådå

Fig. 29 Aswåtåmå

    *Bambang Aswåtåmå* is the only son of Dahjang Durnå by the heavenly nymph Déwi Wilutåmå. He is among the most powerful and important members of the younger generation of the Left faction, but the Gods have ordained that he will not die on the battlefield. He is destined to carry on his father's vendetta with Tjempålåredjå and wreak vengeance on the Pendåwå. Aswåtåmå shares his father's shrewdness and cynicism. He consistently warns Sujudånå that his queen, Déwi Banowati, is working against him, but the King always refuses to listen to what he regards as groundless slander. On the night after the Bråtåjudå is over, he creeps into the Pendåwå camp and takes revenge by stabbing Banowati in her sleep, as well as Drestådjumenå, Srikandi, and Påntjåwålå (see above under *Drupådå*, p. 53). Only when he tries to murder Ardjunå's grandson, the infant Parikesit, does fortune turn against him.

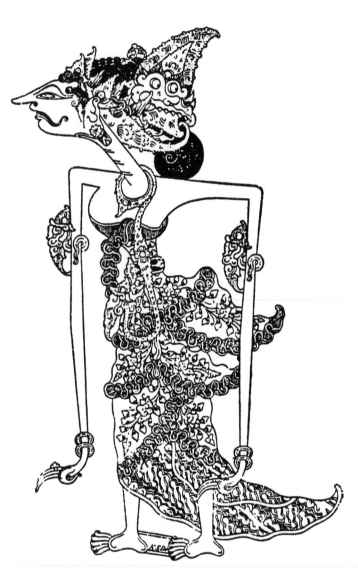

Fig. 30 Banowati

*Déwi Banowati* is the youngest daughter of Prabu Salyå and Sujudånå's queen in Ngastinå. Her proud bearing is indicated by her uptilted nose and scornful smile. Before her arranged marriage with Sujudånå, she and Ardjunå were secretly in love. According to many versions, this affair persisted afterwards, and Banowati is instrumental in betraying the military secrets of Ngastinå to its enemies. After Sujudånå's death Ardjunå takes her as his wife. But their happiness lasts only one night, for Aswåtåmå, Durnå's son, creeping into the Pendåwå camp, murders her in her sleep. Banowati is an ambiguous figure since, although she helps the Pendåwå, she does it by betraying her lawful husband.

Fig. 31 Lesmånå Måndråkumårå

*Radèn Lesmånå Måndråkumårå* is the only son of Sujudånå and Banowati and heir to the throne of Ngastinå. Many of the *lakons* concern the desperate attempts of Prabu Sujudånå to find Lesmånå a wife. Invariably one of the more attractive Pendåwå clan manages to charm or carry off the intended bride, so that the Kuråwå are left empty-handed. Sujudånå's difficulties are compounded by the fact that Lesmånå is cowardly, vain, weak, and a bit soft-headed. He is regarded as a laughing-stock, even in Ngastinå, a spoiled Crown Prince whose thoughts run only to food and women. Lesmånå is killed early in the Bråtåjudå by Ardjunå's son, Abimanju.

Fig. 32 Sangkuni

*Patih Arjå Sangkuni* is usually regarded as the evil genius of the Kuråwå, with loyalty to his King his one redeeming feature. As Dreståråtå's brother-in-law and Sujudånå's uncle, he has the position of Chief Minister of Ngastinå, of which, in view of his nephew's inexperience, he takes full advantage. The cunning stratagems which cause the Pendåwå so much misery and misfortune are all devised by this sly old man. He suffers a terrible end in the Bråtåjudå, having his jaws torn apart by the furious talons of Wrekudårå.

Fig. 33 Dursåsånå

*Radèn Dursåsånå*, the second of the ninety-nine Kuråwå brothers, is regarded as, next to Sangkuni, the most unpleasant of the Left faction. Noisy, boastful, violent, and unscrupulous, he is nevertheless devoted to his elder brother, Sujudånå, and to the fortunes of his clan. In the field, he is a brave fighter, and only the invincible Wrekudårå can destroy him. His role is very important, since at every juncture in the *lakons* it is Dursåsånå and Sangkuni who push the action forward towards a new climax. Each time a settlement appears possible, it is these two who ensure its failure.

*Radèn Djâjâdrâtâ* is a powerful champion of the Kurâwâ. There is some mystery about his origin. The story goes that when Wrekudârâ was born, the caul in which he was wrapped was thrown away. The aged ascetic, Begawan Sapwani, came upon it by chance, prayed over it, and transformed it into a boy-child, who grew up under the name of Djâjâdrâtâ. The family resemblance to Wrekudârâ and Wrekudârâ's son, Radèn Gatutkâtjâ, was obvious from the first. When Djâjâdrâtâ came to manhood he was persuaded to come to Ngastinâ by the astute Sangkuni, who foresaw the need of such an ally against the Pendâwâ. There Djâjâdrâtâ was given a high position and Sujudânâ's sister, Dèwi Dursilowati, as his bride. This bound him firmly to the Left faction. In the Brâtâjudâ, it is he who kills the young Abimanju, only to be killed in turn by the bereaved Ardjunâ. Djâjâdrâtâ's character is honest, loyal, and straightforward—a sort of Gatutkâtjâ among the Kurâwâ.

Fig. 34 Djâjâdrâtâ

Fig. 35 Burisråwå

*Radèn Burisråwå* is one of the most prominent younger leaders of the Kuråwå. He is the eldest son of Prabu Salyå and much feared for his gigantic size and violent, unbridled nature. He falls desperately in love with Sumbådrå, Ardjunå's wife, and many are the *lakons* which deal with his attempts to win possession of her. He swears never to look at another woman if he cannot have her, and indeed he dies without wife or child.

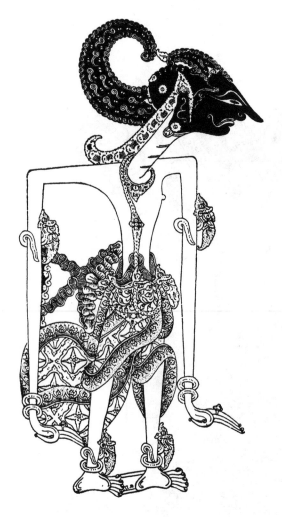

Fig. 36 Nangkulå-Sadéwå

*Radèn Nangkulå* and *Radèn Sadéwå* are twins, the youngest of the Pendåwå. Their mother is not Kunti, but Prabu Salyå's sister, Madrim. Generally speaking, they assume a very subordinate role as followers and emissaries of their older brothers, without evincing any particular characteristics aside from the normal traits of well-behaved young *satryå*. In the Bråtåjudå, it is their mission to discover the secret of their uncle Salyå's invincibility.

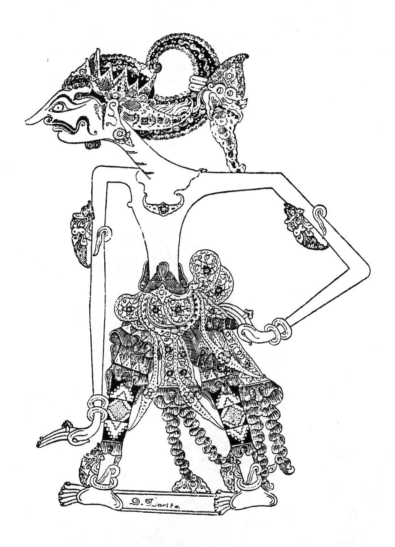

Fig. 37 Setyaki

*Radèn Setyaki*, as first cousin of the Pendåwå and Prabu Kresnå, is one of the stalwarts of the Right. He usually acts as Kresnå's companion and confidant. It is he who joins the lord of Dwåråwati on his last diplomatic mission to Ngastinå. He is very powerful, in spite of his small size, and so is often referred to as the Dwarf Wrekudårå or *Bimå Kunting*. In the Bråtåjudå itself, he is matched with the gigantic Burisråwå and is only saved from death by Kresnå's cunning. He is regarded by the Javanese as the type of the straightforward, brave, diminutive *satryå*.

*Radèn Abimanju (Ångkåwidjåjå)* (see Fig. 4, p. 22) is Ardjunå's son by Sumbådrå and his only legal heir, as Srikandi is childless. Abimanju himself has no children by his marriage to Kresnå's daughter, Déwi Sitisundari; but by Utari, princess of Wiråtå, Parikesit is born to continue to Pendåwå line into historic times. Abimanju is the epitome of the handsome, refined, gentle, but brave young *satryå*, respectful of his elders and always obedient to their wishes. He is Gatutkåtjå's bosom-friend, and the two generally seek adventures together. The *lakon* describing his death is regarded by the Javanese as the most poignant of the Bråtåjudå series. Not only does Abimanju suffer a cruel fate on the battlefield, but his young widow, Sitisundari, immolates herself on her dead husband's funeral pyre.

Fig. 38 Togog

*Radèn Gatutkåtjå* (see Fig. 20, page 44) is Wrekudårå's son by the giantess, Déwi Arimbi. He rules a kingdom of (good) giants in Pringgandani but is always ready to act as the loyal, unhesitatingly obedient agent of his Pendåwå uncles. His special attribute is his ability to fly. President Sukarno has thus referred to him as the first Indonesian astronaut. His romantic passion for Déwi Pregiwå is the subject of one of the most famous *lakons* of all. In the Bråtåjudå he is the last major figure to die on the Pendåwå side, struck down by his uncle, Adipati Karnå, as he flies high above the Kuråwå armies.

*Togog* is reputedly Semar's elder brother, and normally he acts as *punåkawan* to the Left faction. Like Semar he is immortal, and his strange, grotesque shape betrays his supernatural origin. In character he has none of Semar's gentleness and kindly wisdom. His wit is coarser and more cynical. Because his masters are constantly being killed off by the Pendåwå and their children, Togog always appears in a different King's retinue. So he has become the proverbial prototype of the unfaithful, mercenary servant.

Fig. 39 Garèng

*Garèng*, the second of the Pendåwå *punåkawan*, is generally thought to be Semar's eldest son. He is a deformed dwarf, with crooked, disjointed arms, and has yaws sores on his feet. He specializes in puns and sly insinuations rather than in slapstick. Like Semar (see Fig. 17, p. 37) and Pétruk (see Fig. 40, p. 66), he is really immortal and accompanies each generation of the Pendåwå family on their innumerable wanderings and adventures.

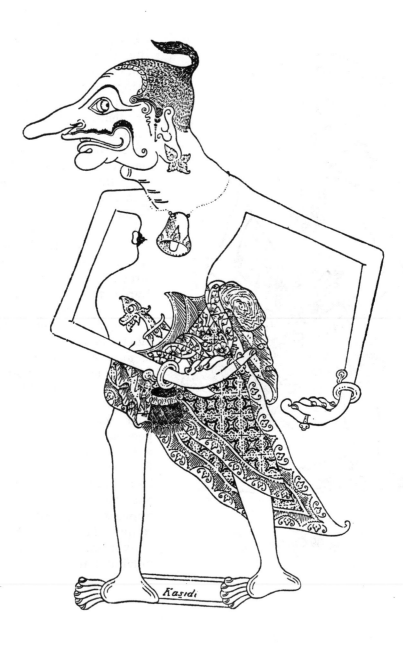

Fig. 40 Pétruk

*Pétruk* is the third of the *punåkawan* in attendance on the Pendåwå and often regarded as Semar's second son. He is notable for his scrawny build, huge, predatory mouth, and long, inquisitive nose. His special delights (and those usually of the audience) are practical jokes and comic horseplay. But when called upon in need he is a redoubtable (because totally unscrupulous) fighter.

Fig. 41 Bagong

*Bagong*, fourth of the Pendåwå *punåkawan*, formerly rarely, if ever, appeared with Garèng and Pétruk. The traditional pattern was that the trio of Semar, Garèng, and Pétruk was popular in Central and East Java, while the duo of Semar and Bagong was the special favorite of Banjumas and West Java. Today they are frequently shown all four together. Bagong has his share of the typical *punåkawan* deformities, a bald head, a hernia, a bulging fat belly and behind, and virtually no nose. His peculiar characteristics are an immensely deep slow voice and impenetrable stupidity, usually taking the form of persistent misunderstanding of what his master or his fellow *punåkawan* have to say.

*Tjangik* is a fa-
vorite comic female ser-
vant, generally in atten-
dance on Sumbâdrâ or some
other high-ranking
princess. In spite of her
emaciated figure, shriv-
eled breasts, and grotesque
features, she is extremely
coy and vain, as the comb
she constantly carries about
with her testifies. Her
voice is high, shrill, and
whistling, as she has no
teeth.

*Limbuk* is Tjangik's
daughter, also a comic female attendant. Though
her appearance differs
strongly from her mother's,
she has the same deter-
mined sense of her own superior attractions. She too
carries a comb with her
everywhere. Her voice is
loud, low, and oddly
touching.

Fig. 42 Tjangik

Fig. 43 Limbuk

Fig. 44 Tjakil

Fig. 45 Térong

*Butå Tjakil* is the favorite antagonist of Ardjunå and his numerous sons in the less serious *lakons*. Each time he is killed, only to reappear again in another story. He is instantly recognizable by his flat head, squinting eyes, and jutting, horn-like tooth. Unlike the other *butå*, he is quite small. In fact, his body is that of a *satryå* and only his extraordinary head betrays his *butå* origin.

*Butå Térong*, the Egg-plant Giant, is so named because his nose closely resembles an aubergine. He is the normal *butå* antagonist for the larger heroes, such as Wrekudårå, while Tjakil is the appropriate adversary for the smaller and more elegant *satryå*. Butå Térong has no defined role in the *lakons* but regularly appears to test the courage and military prowess of the Pendåwå.

*Garudå* is a generic name for a mythological "eagle." There are a number of different characters in the *lakons* who are portrayed with this puppet, the best-known being Djataju in the Ramayana and Wilmukå (the aerial steed of Prabu Kresnå's eldest son, Prabu Bomå) in the Mahabharata. In the one case the puppet represents a bird of great courage, faithfulness, and honor, in the other a creature consumed with jealousy and malice.

Fig. 46 Garudå

*Djuruméjå* is a type of *sétan*, indestructible, malevolent spirit, who serves in the palace of Betari Durgå at Sétrågåndåmaju. The Goddess regularly sends Djuruméjå and his fellow-*sétan* to confuse, torment, and terrify the Pendåwå, usually with great success. It requires the special powers of Semar to put the evil spirits to flight.

Fig. 47 Djuruméjå

Fig. 48 Brahålå

*Brahålå* is the name given to Kresnå when he assumes his terrible World-Destroyer manifestation, the *triwikråmå*.

# APPENDIX II
# MAHABHARATA:
# A JAVANESE VERSION
# ACCORDING TO THE *LAKONS*

For many years Prabu Abjåså had ruled the great kingdom of Ngastinå in justice, peace, and prosperity. Yet the king had his own private sorrow. Each of his three sons was tragically afflicted. The eldest, Dreståråtå, was blind, the second, Pandu, was an albino, while the third, Widurå, was incurably lame. In the course of time the aging monarch decided to abdicate and spend his last years in religious meditation and ascesis. Since his blindness was felt to bar Dreståråtå from the succession, Abjåså named Pandu ruler of Ngastinå, with the understanding that the throne would later revert to Dreståråtå's line. Nevertheless there were many who felt that Pandu, once crowned sovereign King, was entitled to designate his own successor. This was the origin of the bitter feud between the sons of Dreståråtå (the Kuråwå) and the sons of Pandu (the Pendåwå), which was only to be settled by the Last War, the Bråtåjudå Djåjåbinangun.

The Kuråwå consisted of ninety-nine boys and one girl, Déwi Dursilowati, born to Dreståråtå by his wife, Gendari. Eldest of them all was Kurupati, who was eventually to become King of Ngastinå. Next came the violent Dursåsånå, Tjitrakså, Tjitraksi, and then all the others. When they came of age, the children of Dreståråtå contracted two dynastic alliances of great importance. Kurupati married Déwi Banowati, daughter of the celebrated King of Mandråkå, Prabu Salyå; and Dursilowati's hand was given to the powerful and respected prince, Radèn Djåjådråtå.

The Pendåwå, five in number, were all boys. The three eldest, Judistirå, Wrekudårå, and Ardjunå, were the children of Pandu's first wife, Déwi Kunti Nalibråtå. The two youngest, Nangkulå and Sadéwå, were twins born to Pandu's second wife, Déwi Madrim, sister of Prabu Salyå. Although Pandu was ostensibly their father, he had in fact been cursed with impotency, and the children were all sired by Gods—Judistirå by Batårå Darmå, Wrekudårå by Sang Hyang Baju, Ardjunå by Batårå Éndrå, and the twins by the two Aswis. Like the Kuråwå, the young Pendåwå won important allies by marriage. Judistirå and Ardjunå respectively married Déwi Drupadi and Déwi Srikandi, the daughters of Prabu Drupådå of Tjempålåredjå, and sisters of Radèn Drestådjumenå. Ardjunå's other bride, Déwi Sumbådrå, was not only his own first cousin but also the sister of Prabu Kresnå, the powerful lord of Dwåråwati.

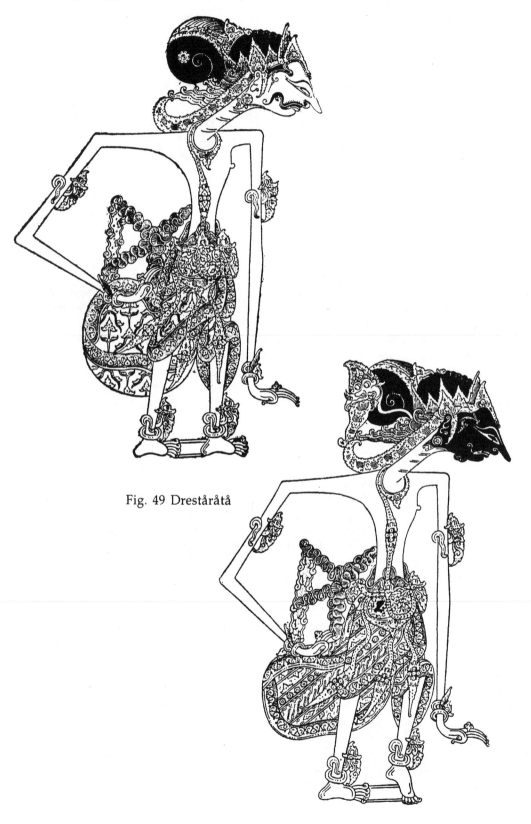

Fig. 49 Dreståråtå

Fig. 50 Widurå

Fig. 51 Kunti

Fig. 52 Drupadi

Now, before her marriage to Pandu, Déwi Kunti Nalibråtå had had a child by Batårå Suryå, the Sun God. Her father, ashamed of his daughter's untimely pregnancy, put the newborn baby into a casket and set it afloat on a nearby river. The child, a boy, was rescued by a humble charioteer and given the name Karnå. When a young man, his military skill, aristocratic bearing, and nobility of character caught the eye of Kurupati. Hoping for support in his continuing rivalry with Pandu's sons, the eldest of the Kuråwå encouraged and befriended the young Karnå, little knowing who he really was. Thus it was that Kunti's first-born son came to be arrayed on the side of her younger children's mortal enemies.

Pandu himself did not rule for long in Ngastinå. He died while both Kuråwå and Pendåwå were still small children. Dreståråtå, once passed over for the succession, became regent till their maturity. Both Kuråwå and Pendåwå were brought up together at Ngastinå under the watchful eyes of Dahjang Durnå, the subtle *brahmånå*, and the aged Resi Bhismå. Dreståråråtå's infirmity prevented him from ruling in more than name, and effective power passed increasingly to these two and to Dreståråtå's brother-in-law and Chief Minister, the cunning Sangkuni.

From the beginning, the cousins were in constant and embittered rivalry, which came to a climax when Dreståråtå decided to abdicate in favor of his son, Kurupati, who then ascended the throne as Prabu Sujudånå. The Pendåwå felt that their claims had been unjustly disregarded, while the Kuråwå, in spite of their numbers, feared that their position would never be secure so long as their more gifted, God-favored cousins remained alive to challenge them. Love, as well as politics, became a source of strife. Sujudånå suffered the humiliation of having his wife won for him by Ardjunå, most irresistible of Javanese princes. Indeed, even after her marriage to the new King of Ngastinå, Déwi Banowati remained enamored of Ardjunå and he of her—a fact which did not fail further to poison relations between the cousins.

It was, however, the Chief Minister, Sangkuni, who, either out of fear for his own position, affection for his nephews, or some innate instinct for mischief, blew on the smoldering rivalry between the cousins until it flared into open conflict. Working on the young Sujudånå's anxieties, he persuaded him to invite the five Pendåwå and their mother, Kunti, to a formal conference, ostensibly to discuss the division of the kingdom into two—one half for Judistirå and his brothers and one for the Kuråwå. Suspecting no guile, the Pendåwå appeared and were lodged in a beautiful pavilion, specially constructed of inflammable lacquer. After a lavish and convivial banquet, the Pendåwå retired to bed, all except the watchful Wrekudårå. Now came their limping uncle, Widurå, warning his nephews of Kuråwå treachery and advising them in case of need to follow a white civet. Soon afterwards agents of Sangkuni set the lacquer pavilion afire, hoping to trap the sleeping Pendåwå in the holocaust. But Déwi Kunti and her five sons, led by Wrekudårå, discovered a mysterious white civet suddenly before them and escaped death by following it down a subterranean passage and eventually, after various adventures, up again into a remote, desolate forest.

In fear of their lives, the Pendåwå now came to the court of Prabu Matswåpati, King of Wiråtå, where, in disguise, they sought employment. Judistirå became a learned *brahmånå*, Wrekudårå a butcher, Ardjunå an eunuch dancing-master, and the twins herdsmen. Though the Kuråwå searched high and low they could find no trace of them. In time, however, the danger passed and the secret of their identity was made known to Matswåpati.

With Matswåpati's help and that of Ardjunå's cousin and brother-in-law Prabu Kresnå, the Pendåwå cleared a wide space in the forest where they had first taken refuge and there built a magnificent palace which they called Ngamartå. Now Judistirå was crowned King, and a period of glory and prosperity ensued. From all sides people came to settle under the wise and humane rule of the gentle Pendåwå. But the rivalry with the Kuråwå continued. The Pendåwå never abandoned their claims, nor the Kuråwå their fears. To the ranks of the Kuråwå was now added Prabu Salyå's gigantic son, Radèn Burisråwå, who, desperate for love of Déwi Sumbådrå, swore that if he could not marry her he would never touch another woman. Since Sumbådrå was already Ardjunå's wife and had even borne him a child, Radèn Abimanju, only Ardjunå's death could accomplish Burisråwå's purpose.

The growing glory and renown of Ngamartå was a burning thorn in the heart of Sujudånå, and once again he turned to his uncle, Sangkuni, for advice. The cunning Chief Minister suggested that he invite the Pendåwå for a feast of reconciliation and there prevail upon Judistirå to play at dice. This was the King of Ngamartå's single weakness, and Sangkuni's special skill. Once again the Pendåwå fell into the trap that had been prepared for them. They came to the feast and Judistirå agreed to gamble with Sangkuni, though his brothers all warned him of danger. As the hours passed, Judistirå progressively lost all his material possessions then his kingdom, later his own freedom, and finally that of his brothers and even his wife, Déwi Drupadi. The Pendåwå were struck dumb by the disaster which had overtaken them. The Kuråwå were overjoyed, and Dursåsånå moved to take possession of Drupadi, tearing open her gown at the thigh and pulling loose her bound-up hair. Trembling with rage, Drupadi reminded the Kuråwå that, having already given up his own freedom, her husband could not legally stake that of his wife or brothers, so that neither she nor the other Pendåwå were bound by the last throws of the dice. Moreover she swore that she would leave her dress torn and her hair unbraided until the day when she could wash her tresses in Dursåsånå's blood. Wrekudårå also cursed the Kuråwå and promised that one day he would tear Dursåsånå limb from limb with his nails and rip Sangkuni's lying jaws apart. Then in silence the Pendåwå departed, stripped of everything they possessed. Sujudånå made no move to stop them, stunned by the terrible scene that had just passed.

Once again the Pendåwå were reduced to nothing. Once again they were forced to wander in lonely poverty through the woods and mountains, attended as always by their faithful clown-attendants (*punåkawan*), Semar, Garèng, and Pétruk. Whenever despair settled upon them, their spirits were lightened by the antics of Pétruk and Garèng and their hopes raised by Semar's gentle, wise advice.

Many years again passed by, until the Pendåwå, with the aid of Kresnå and Matswåpati, were able once more to muster their strength. To seal the alliance between the Pendåwå and Wiråtå, Ardjunå's eldest and best-loved son, Radèn Abimanju, was summoned and married to Matswåpati's daughter, Déwi Utari. At the wedding it was foretold that their child would eventually rule a united Java in peace and prosperity and would in turn beget a historic line of Javanese kings. And now the Gods began to give signs that the Last War, Bråtåjudå Djåjåbinangun, was at hand. The Pendåwå decided to send Kresnå to Ngastinå to make one final attempt to settle the long enmity by persuading Sujudånå to yield half his kingdom.

Prabu Kresnå arrived at Ngastinå accompanied only by his cousin and friend, Radèn Setyaki, otherwise known as the Dwarf Wrekudårå (*Bimå Kunting*). Meanwhile, Dahjang Durnå and Patih Aryå Sangkuni had warned Sujudånå that he had no hope of ultimate victory in the Bråtåjudå unless he could destroy Kresnå before it began. With much doubt and uneasiness in his heart, Sujudånå accordingly consented to lay an ambush for Kresnå and Setyaki, although they came under the flag of truce. The conference opened peacefully enough, but neither side would yield in its demands. Then as Kresnå retired to his quarters to rest, Dursåsånå led the palace guard against him. Enraged by this treacherous attack. Kresnå, who was an incarnation of the God Wisnu, suddenly assumed his most terrible, demonic form, the mountain-high, gigantic *Triwikråmå*, with a thousand heads and ten thousand arms and legs. At the very echo of his thunderous voice, the foundations of the palace of Ngastinå were riven. In shrieking panic the Kuråwå sought refuge where they could. But none would have escaped speedy destruction had not the Gods, in the person of Karnå's father, Batårå Suryå, suddenly appeared to warn Kresnå that he was forbidden to shed Kuråwå blood. The Kuråwå were destined for annihilation not at his but at the Pendåwå's hands. Drupadi's curse must work itself out. By the decree of the Gods, Kresnå's role must be limited to acting as the Pendåwå's adviser. The words of the Sun God had their effect. Kresnå resumed his mortal shape. He went to take leave of the Pendåwå's mother, Dèwi Kunti, who remained at Ngastinå, and promised to convey her blessing to her children. Therewith he set off with the faithful Setyaki for Wiråtå, intending to report on the failure of his mission.

Meanwhile, Karnå had been summoned by his mother, who pleaded with him to abandon the Kuråwå and join his brothers at Wiråtå. But he steadfastly refused, reminding his mother that she had abandoned him as a newborn baby. By this act of cruelty she had forfeited all claims to his love and obedience. He owed a deep debt of gratitude to Sujudånå, who had made him what he was, the foremost *satryå* in Ngastinå. Nevertheless, he acknowledged his shame at Sujudånå's treacherous attack on Kresnå and his foreboding that Ngastinå was doomed. He promised his mother finally that he would fight with none of his brothers but Ardjunå. Thus, regardless of who won that fateful duel, Kunti would still have five sons left. Leaving his mother in tears, Karnå then rode homewards to his palace at Ngawånggå. On the way he encountered Kresnå, and for a time the two rode on together side by side. Like Kunti, Kresnå tried to persuade Karnå to change his mind and side with the Pendåwå but with no better success. They then parted amicably, and each went his own way.

When Kresnå had related what had occurred at Ngastinå, the decision was taken to go to war. The Pendåwå now gathered their allies together at Wiråtå. Aside from the five brothers themselves, the assembled heroes included Prabu Kresnå from Dwåråwati, his son, Radèn Såmbå, and his Chief Minister, Udåwå; Prabu Matswåpati of Wiråtå and his three sons, Radèn Sétå, Radèn Utårå, and Radèn Wratsångkå; Prabu Drupådå of Tjempålåredjå and his son, Radèn Drestådjumenå; Ardjunå's heir, Radèn Abimanju, and Wrekudårå's son, Radèn Gatutkåtjå, among many others. When all preparations had been made, the Pendåwå armies marched forward to the place of battle, the great plain to be known later as *Tegal Kurusétrå* (Burial-Field of the Kuråwå).

To Ngastinå there came word of the preparations at Wiråtå. Prabu Sujudånå too now gathered together his friends and allies. Among them came his father-in-law, Prabu Salyå, with the armies of Mandråkå; his brothers-in-law, Radèn Djåjådråtå and Radèn Burisråwå; Dahjang Durnå, Resi Bhismå, Adipati Karnå, and many others. An appeal was sent to Kresnå's invincible brother, Prabu Bålådéwå of Mandurå, whose wife was also a daughter of Prabu Salyå, and who usually defended the Kuråwå cause. But Kresnå had already foreseen this danger. Knowing that if Bålådéwå fought for the Kuråwå all would be lost, he persuaded his brother to go into a deep trance in preparation for the fighting, promising him that he would be awakened when the Bråtåjudå was to begin. In fact, he intended only to waken him when the Kuråwå had finally been destroyed. Thus the Kuråwå mission to Mandurå met with no success.

The two armies now faced each other across the wind-swept plain. After rites of great solemnity and splendor, hostilities were engaged.

On the first day, Resi Bhismå led the Kuråwå forces to victory. Matswåpati's three sons, Sétå, Utårå, and Wratsångkå, all perished at his hands, and Sujudånå was overcome with joy. When darkness fell, Kresnå warned the despondent Pendåwå that, when he was a young man, Resi Bhismå had accidentally killed a certain Déwi Ambalikå, who was in love with him. As she lay dying she had sworn to return and have her revenge. Now Ambalikå had reincarnated herself in Ardjunå's warrior-wife, Srikandi, and through Srikandi alone could Bhismå be overcome. Accordingly, it was agreed by all the Pendåwå chiefs that on the next day Srikandi should lead their forces into battle.

On the second day, as Kresnå had foreseen, Bhismå encountered Srikandi and recognized that his hour had come. Without resistance he allowed himself to be pierced by her arrows. As he lay dying, the fighting stopped, and both sides came to pay their respects to the fallen hero and ask for his blessing. With his last breath he prophesied victory for the Pendåwå and ruin for their rivals.

On the third day, Durnå's cunning persuaded the Pendåwå's mightiest champions, Ardjunå and Wrekudårå, to engage in single combat far from the battlefield with two of Sujudånå's lesser allies. Durnå's plan was to take advantage of their absence to deal a decisive blow. Into the breach now stepped Ardjunå's son, Abimanju. Leading the counterattack, he succeeded in cutting down Sujudånå's only son and heir, Radèn Lesmånå Måndråkumårå. But his inexperience was his undoing. The Kuråwå pretended to give ground and drew him into their midst. There he was surrounded, pierced with arrows, and finally clubbed to death by Radèn Djåjådråtå. When the faithful Semar brought the news to Ardjunå, the bereaved father almost took leave of his senses, wandering pathetically back towards the battlefield calling for his son, without thought of danger. But finally Kresnå roused him from his grief to thoughts of revenge, and he swore to destroy Djåjådråtå before sundown or himself mount the ritual pyre where his son's dead body lay. Word of this solemn oath spread rapidly to the Kuråwå camp. On Sangkuni's advice, Djåjådråtå was hidden where none could find him. The long day passed while Ardjunå hunted for his chosen adversary in vain. As the sun declined, he prepared to immolate himself in grief, shame, and despair. But now Kresnå used his magic weapon, the Tjåkrå, to darken the sky so completely that it seemed as if night had already fallen. The Kuråwå were deceived and the jubilant Djåjådråtå now emerged from concealment to witness Ardjunå's death by fire. Immediately the

Tjåkrå was withdrawn, and in the red light of sunset Ardjunå's arrow sped unerringly to its mark in Djåjådråtå's throat.

On the fourth day, Radèn Burisråwå was challenged by Radèn Setyaki. The battle went badly for the diminutive hero, and he was about to be crushed to death when his cousin Kresnå intervened, urging Ardjunå to shoot Burisråwå down from behind. Ardjunå, however, refused, saying that it was against the *satryå* code for an onlooker to interfere in a single combat of this kind. Undismayed, Kresnå resorted to a stratagem. He held up a fine hair between Ardjunå and Burisråwå and asked if Ardjunå could split it with an arrow. Ardjunå innocently agreed to try, and indeed succeeded in dividing the hair. But the arrow flew on and lodged itself deep in Burisråwå's heart. Bitterly shamed, Ardjunå retired for the day from the field of battle. His place was taken by Wrekudårå's winged son, Radèn Gatutkåtjå, who now led the Pendåwå against the Kuråwå forces under Adipati Karnå. A terrible battle developed, in which Karnå was finally forced to make use of his most magical arrow, Kjai Kontå, to bring down the flying hero. The Kuråwå were overjoyed at Gatutkåtjå's death. But this was to be their last triumph.

The fifth day proved to be the climax of the great war, for Ardjunå and Karnå finally met face to face. Prabu Salyå was Karnå's charioteer, Prabu Kresnå Ardjunå's. Both heroes hesitated at first, but Kresnå reminded Ardjunå of his obligations as a *satryå* and of Gatutkåtjå's death the previous day at Karnå's hands. Then the battle was joined, and for long neither side had the advantage, being perfectly matched. Then, seeing an opportunity, Karnå launched his most terrifying arrow. But Salyå, humiliated that he had been forced to act as his son-in-law's charioteer and in his heart siding with the Pendåwå, suddenly jerked the reins and brought his horses to their knees. Thus the blazing arrow passed through Ardjunå's hair and not his head. Then Ardjunå unleashed his own magical arrow, Pasopati, and Karnå fell to his death in the dust.

On the sixth day, the aged Durnå led the Kuråwå to battle in Karnå's place. Ardjunå refused to fight his old teacher, and the other Pendåwå proved no match for the old *brahmånå*'s magical arts. Only when Kresnå ordered Wrekudårå to kill an elephant bearing the same name as Durnå's son, Bambang Aswåtåmå, and Judistirå was induced to convince the old man that it was indeed his son who had died, did it become possible to win the day. Transfixed in silent grief, the once invincible *brahmånå* was an easy prey to the rash Drestådjumenå, who lopped off his head although he offered no resistance. From afar, Aswåtåmå witnessed what had happened and swore to have his revenge.

On the seventh day, Prabu Salyå guided the Kuråwå to temporary victory with his irresistible weapon, the Tjåndåbiråwå. The Pendåwå armies scattered in panic, suffering heavy losses. Kuråwå hopes were unexpectedly raised. But when night fell, Kresnå sent the twins, Nangkulå and Sadéwå, sons of Salyå's beloved sister, Madrim, to seek out the secret of Salyå's power. Prabu Salyå, who had never approved of Sujudånå's actions but had joined him out of family loyalty, told the young men that he could only be vanquished by a king whose blood ran white.

Accordingly, on the eighth day, Judistirå, purest of mortals, led the Pendåwå to battle, though he had never in his life raised a hand in violence. He brought with him no destructive weapon, only his sacred heirloom, the holy text Kalimåsådå. Now the Tjåndåbiråwå's power was shattered. The ghost of Begawan Bagaspati, the *rasekså* hermit whom Salyå had killed so as to marry his daughter, Déwi Satyåwati, appeared in the air, hovering over the battlefield.

Promising revenge, the ghost vanished into the body of Judistirå. Suddenly transformed into a menacing warrior, the eldest Pendåwå now advanced to the fray and immediately brought Salyå low with Ardjunå's magic arrow, the Pasopati.

On the ninth day, the curse of Drupadi worked itself out. Wrekudårå encountered Dursåsånå, and, after a murderous struggle, he tore his cousin limb from limb with his terrible nails, the Påntjånåkå. Drupadi appeared on the field of battle and bathed her locks in the dying man's blood. Sangkuni then advanced but proved no match for the enraged, gigantic Wrekudårå, who snatched him up bodily and tore his jaws apart.

On the tenth and last day, Sujudånå was left alone to face Wrekudårå in single combat. So great was his valor and strength that Wrekudårå could not prevail until Kresnå signaled him to strike a foul blow on Sujudånå's thigh. The great King of Ngastinå then sank to the ground in agony, there to fall helpless victim to the Påntjånåkå. And now it happened that Bålådéwå had at last been awakened from his trance by the thunder of battle and hurried to the Tegal Kurusétrå in time to witness Sujudånå's end. He bitterly reproached Kresnå for his deceit and for the ignoble ruse which had brought the last of the Kuråwå to his downfall. Unmoved, Kresnå replied that he was merely carrying out the will of the Gods.

In somber mood the Pendåwå now approached the fallen city of Ngastinå. At the gates they found Gendari, mother of the Kuråwå, sunk in desperate brief. Of all her hundred children, not one was left alive. In her despair she turned on Kresnå and cursed him with a mother's curse. She foretold that he himself would lose all his own children first and at the end die miserable, forsaken, and alone, shot by a woodcutter's arrow in a remote and desolate forest.

The Pendåwå now took their rest. But Durnå's son, Bambang Aswåtåmå, who had fled the field of battle, stole back into Ngastinå by night to seek revenge. As they slept, he stabbed to death Radèn Drestådjumenå, Déwi Srikandi, Drupadi's son, Radèn Påntjåwålå, and Sujudånå's widow, Banowati, who had happily rejoined her first love, Ardjunå, after her husband's death. He also attempted to kill Parikesit, Ardjunå's little grandson, but the baby had been sleeping with the sprung Pasopati at his feet. Startled by the midnight intruder, the infant stirred. The arrow, released, flew from the bow, and Aswåtåmå fell mortally wounded at the crib-side.

Dawn came, and the night's slaughter was discovered. Stricken, the Pendåwå decided to depart. Kresnå returned to Dwåråwati with Setyaki and Udåwå. Bålådéwå was left to guard and rear the young Parikesit (see Fig. 53, page 84), who would one day rule over a new Ngastinå. The five brothers, accompanied by Drupadi and a faithful hound, set off for the Universal Mountain, the Måhåméru. But, weighed down bythe blood that had been shed, their strength faded as they ascended the holy mountain towards heaven. One by one they fell exhausted by the wayside, first Drupadi, then Sadéwå, Nangkulå, Ardjunå, and finally even Wrekudårå. Only the saintly Judistirå reached the gate of Heaven. There he was invited to enter, alone, but he refused so long as his wife, his brothers, and his hound were compelled to remain outside. The Gods relented, and the whole company passed up into the celestial sphere, their task on earth now at last accomplished.

Fig. 53 Parikesit

# APPENDIX III
# GENEALOGIES OF THE MAHABHARATA
# (JAVANESE VERSION)

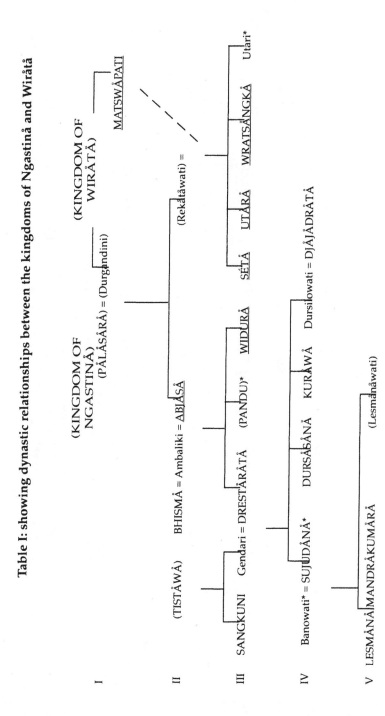

Table I: showing dynastic relationships between the kingdoms of Ngastinå and Wiråtå

(For Legend, see Table II)

**Table II: showing relationship between the kingdom of Mandråkå and leading figures of the Kuråwå**

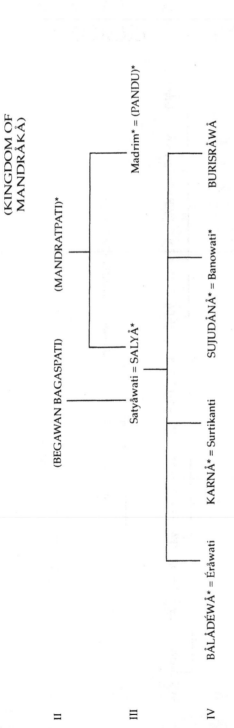

(KINGDOM OF MANDRÅKÅ)

II

(BEGAWAN BAGASPATI)          (MANDRATPATI)*

Madrim* = (PANDU)*

III

Satyåwati = SALYÅ*

IV

BÅLÅDÉWÅ* = Érawati          KARNÅ* = Surtikanti          SUJUDÅNÅ* = Banowati*          BURISRÅWÅ

*Legend*   I   Numbers in the left-hand margin indicate generations, and are included to help in correlating the four genealogical tables

Ambaliki        Small type indicates that the person is feminine
SANGKUNI        Large type indicates that the person is masculine
(PÅLÅSÅRÅ)      Parentheses indicate that the person plays no active role in the main drama
Utari*          Asterisk indicates that the person appears again in another genealogical table
ABIÅSÅ          Underlining indicates association with the Pendåwå faction, and lack of underlining indicates
BHISMÅ          association with the Kurawa

# Table III: showing dynastic relationships between the kingdoms of Ngamartå, Mandurå, and Dwåråwati

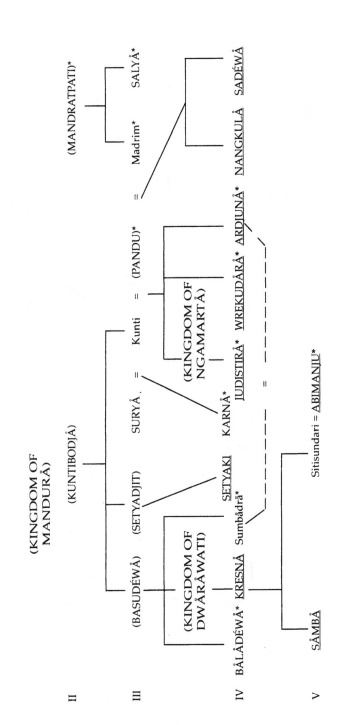

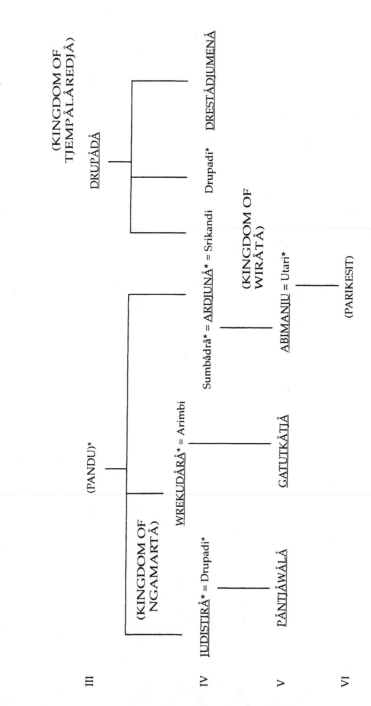

Table IV: showing dynastic relationships between the kingdoms of Ngamartå, Tjempålåredjå, and Wiråtå

# APPENDIX IV
# RAMAYANA: A JAVANESE VERSION ACCORDING TO THE *LAKONS*

Fig. 54 Dåsåmukå

For years a deep enmity had festered between Prabu Dåsåråtå, lord of Ngajodyå, and the giant Prabu Dåsåmukå, ruler of the island kingdom of Ngalengkå. Twice the kings had been rivals in love, once for Déwi Raguwati, once for Déwi Kékaji. Twice Dåsåråtå had prevailed, though less through valor and strength than through cunning and the favor of the Gods. In his disappointment Dåsåmukå swore to take revenge.

In time a new generation grew up in the two royal capitals. In Ngalengkå, Dåsåmukå's wife, a heavenly nymph, gave birth to a baby girl in her husband's absence. Dåsåmukå's younger brother, Radèn Wibisånå, took the infant, put it in a casket, and set it afloat on a great river running down to the sea. Eventually the baby was found by the King of the neighboring state of Mantili, who reared the little girl as his own child and gave her the name Déwi Sintå. To prevent Dåsåmukå discovering what had happened, Wibisånå created a boy out of a dark mass of cloud, gave him the name Mégånåndå (Indradjit), and presented him to Dåsåmukå as his son.

Fig. 55 Wibisånå

Fig. 56 Sintå

Fig. 57 Indradjit

Meanwhile, in Ngajodyå, Déwi Raguwati gave birth to two sons, Råmå and Lesmånå. Not long afterwards Déwi Kékaji bore Dåsåråtå a third son, who was named Radèn Baråtå. When the boys had grown to manhood, the news was brought that the King of Mantili would hold a tournament for the hand of his beautiful daughter, Déwi Sintå. Råmå decided to enter the tournament and was brilliantly successful, bringing Sintå home to Ngajodyå as his wife.

Fig. 58 Råmå

Fig. 59 Lesmånå

Soon afterwards, Dåsåråtå, feeling his end approaching, announced his intention of abdicating in favor of his eldest son, Råmå. But Déwi Kékaji, jealous for her own child, Baråtå, began to poison the old man's mind against his designated successor. Råmå proudly refused to defend himself against Kékaji's whispered charges and was therefore banished from the court, followed by Sintå and the faithful Lesmånå. Reminding Dåsåråtå of an earlier promise that she could have one wish which he would fulfill whatever the cost, Déwi Kékaji now compelled her husband to make Baråtå his heir. To her dismay, however, Baråtå himself refused to cooperate with her plans. When Dåsåråtå died, not long after, Baråtå followed after Råmå into the forest in the hope of persuading him to return to Ngajodyå and ascend the throne. But all his entreaties were in vain. Exhausted by his efforts, Baråtå fell asleep in his tent; and in the middle of the night Råmå, Sintå, and Lesmånå disappeared without leaving a trace. Disconsolately Baråtå turned back, and eventually he agreed to act as Regent in Ngajodyå until the day of Råmå's homecoming.

Fig. 60 Sarpåkenåkå

Meanwhile the exiles found shelter in a remote hermitage, deep in the forest. Here one day Dåsåmukå's younger sister, Déwi Sarpåkenåkå, happened to pass by and fell immediately and desperately in love with the ascetic, celibate Lesmånå. He rejected her frank advances and reproached her bitingly for her immodesty. Furious at her persistence, he finally cut off her nose and her ears. In a fury, Sarpåkenåkå returned to Ngalengkå and complained to her brother that she had been wantonly insulted by Dåsåråtå's sons. Dåsåmukå now saw a chance to have his revenge on the children of his old enemy. Acting on Sarpåkenåkå's report of what she had seen, he sent her husband, his trusted servant Maritjå, to tempt Déwi Sintå by assuming the form of a golden hart. The ruse succeeded beyond expectation. On seeing the beautiful animal, Sintå immediately asked Råmå to catch it for her. Maritjå then cunningly drew Råmå further and further into the woods. After a time, uneasy at her husband's continued absence, Sintå insisted that Lesmånå go to find him, although Råmå had expressly forbidden his younger brother to leave her unguarded. Embarrassed by her urgency, Lesmånå very unwillingly set off. Now Dåsåmukå appeared in the guise of an aged ascetic and successfully lured Sintå out of the magic circle in which Råmå had placed her. Seizing her in his arms, the Giant-King bore her aloft and flew back towards Ngalengkå. The Garuda-eagle, Djataju, seeing what had happened, sped to the unlucky Sintå's rescue. But he was no match for Dåsåmukå and finally fell to earth, mortally wounded.

Radèn Råmå, meantime, irked by his inability to catch the golden hart unharmed, shot it down with his unerring arrows. To his astonishment and dismay, the dying beast suddenly changed into a giant. Maritjå, wounded to death had resumed his natural form. Filled with anxiety and foreboding, Råmå hurried home to the hermitage. On the way he met Lesmånå, and together the brothers discovered that Sintå had completely vanished in their absence. Drawn by distant moans, they soon found the dying Djataju, who revealed to them the identity of Sintå's abductor.

On their journey to Ngalengkå, the brothers first encountered the White Ape, Hanoman, son of the Wind God, Batårå Baju, who had been sent by the Lord of Heaven, Batårå Guru, to give them aid. He counseled them first to seek allies for the struggle against Dåsåmukå. Soon they came to the Kingdom of the Apes, where a bitter contest for the throne was raging between Sugriwå (see Fig. 62, page 96) and Subali. On Hanoman's advice, Råmå came to Sugriwå's rescue by shooting Subali through the heart. In gratitude Sugriwå agreed to join the quest for Sintå and to bring the monkey armies with him.

Fig. 61 Hanoman

Fig. 62 Sugriwå

Fig. 63 Tridjåtå

Eventually Råmå reached the shore of the strait which separated the island of Ngalengkå from the mainland. He then decided to send Hanoman ahead to spy out the land. With one mighty leap the White Ape crossed the waters, soon afterwards finding himself in the pleasure-garden where Sintå was being held prisoner by Dåsåmukå. For the Giant-King still disdained to take her by force, hoping against hope that in time she would yield to him of her own accord. Little did he realize that she was in fact his own daughter. Hanoman climbed a tall tree, and soon he observed Sintå conversing with her guardian and friend, Déwi Tridjåtå, Wibisånå's faithful daughter. Slipping quietly into the garden, Hanoman approached the two women and, with Tridjåtå's connivance, addressed himself to Sintå. He told her that help was at last at hand and gave her Råmå's ring as a sign of his love and trust. Sintå in turn gave the ape her own ring to bring back to her husband.

On his homeward journey Hanoman's luck ran out. He was captured by the powerful young Crown Prince of Ngalengkå, Radèn Indradjit and, on Dåsåmukå's orders, condemned to be burned alive as a spy. At this juncture, Radèn Wibisånå and Dåsåmukå's other brother, the gigantic Radèn Kumbåkarnå, intervened, strongly urging the King to return Sintå to her husband and release the White Ape before it was too late. Dåsåmukå's trusted Chief Minister, Prahastå, seconded their advice. But all to no purpose. Incensed by their opposition, Dåsåmukå bade them choose once and for all between himself and Råmå. So long as he lived, he would never surrender the beautiful princess of Mantili. With a heavy heart, Wibisånå then

Fig. 64 Prahastå

declared that he could neither accept Sintå's unlawful abduction nor be a party to the cruel death planned for Hanoman. He deeply believed that justice must come before family loyalty. Dåsåmukå generously granted him permission to leave, and he immediately set off to join Råmå. Kumbåkarnå and Prahaståmade the opposite decision. While disapproving of Dåsåmukå's course of action and warning that the Gods would undoubtedly favor Råmå, they felt in their hearts that they could not abandon their King and so were prepared, if necessary, to die for him. This proof of their disinterested devotion momentarily caused Dåsåmukå to hesitate, but his earlier oath of vengeance, his desire for Sintå, and the renewed complaints of Sarpåkenåkå, who reminded him of her humiliations and the death of the faithful Maritjå, strengthened his resolve to continue the struggle. Kumbåkarnå thereupon immediately retired to a high mountain, where he sank into a deep religious trance, gathering his forces for the coming battle.

Hanoman's tail was then set alight by Dåsåmukå's executioners. But, summoning all his supernatural strength, the White Ape burst his bonds, leapt high into the air, and flew across the glittering capital of Ngalengkå, setting fire to the roof-tops with his flaming tail. Another mighty leap brought him back to Råmå and Lesmånå, to whom he recounted the story of his mission. Learning that Sintå was alive and still unravished by Dåsåmukå, Råmå decided on war. With the help of Sugriwå's apes, who formed a living bridge across the straits, he passed over to Ngalengkå, in spite of the advance armies that Dåsåmukå sent against him.

Now the decisive struggle opened. For days it raged fiercely without any result. Then the tide began to turn. First Sarpåkenåkå, then the loyal Prahaståˌsuccumbed. In desperation Dåsåmukå summoned Kumbåkarnå. But the giant hero was too deeply sunk in meditation to be easily awakened, even though chariots were driven furiously across his colossal frame. Finally Indradjit succeeded in rousing him. Kumbåkarnå then arose, clothed himself in white in recognition of the death he felt approaching, said farewell to his wife and child, and left for the battlefield. Then all Råmå's armies were speedily put to flight. None could withstand the onslaught of Kumbåkarnå's unequaled strength. Sugriwå was hurled to the ground half-dead. His monkey hordes were crushed in their thousands by each giant stride of Kumbåkarnå's feet and each whirl of his titanic arms. Hanoman himself was barely able to hold his own. It was only when the two were locked in a last, mortal combat and Kumbåkarnå appeared on the verge of victory that Lesmånå came to the aid of the White Ape and shot an arrow into Kumbåkarnå's heart. He fell, mortally wounded, to the ground; and it was as if the World-Mountain, the Måhåméru itself, had crashed down from heaven to earth.

The following day, Indradjit was sent out to avenge his uncle's death. So great was his magical power that once again Råmå's army scattered in panic. Lesmånå went to meet him and was at once struck dead in an unequal combat. Hanoman himself proved powerless against this adversary. Then Wibisånå, who had himself created Indradjit, told Råmå the secret of his origin and how his destruction could be accomplished. Råmå then shot his most magically potent arrow, and the terrible Indradjit dissolved into a vast, dark cloud, which rapidly covered the whole sky and blotted out the sun. The battlefield was black as night, and the opposing armies separated in blind confusion.

Prabu Dåsåmukå was now alone. Nevertheless, he was determined to carry on the long struggle. When dawn came he set forth with the remnants of his army. Meanwhile Lesmånå and Sugriwå had been restored to life when Råmå touched their bleeding wounds with the Flower of Life, Widjåjåkusumå. At least Råmå and Dåsåmukå met in single combat. But neither was able to overcome the other. Repeatedly Råmå shot off Dåsåmukå's head from his body with his blazing arrows, but each time Dåsåmukå uttered a magic spell and head and torso were at once reunited. Then Hanoman came to the rescue. As Råmå once again lopped off Prabu Dåsåmukå's head, the White Ape snatched up a mountain-top and cast it down on the headless trunk, covering it completely so that the severed head could never return to its place. Nevertheless, so magically potent was the King of Ngalengkå that he could not wholly die. At times his angry body still stirs and to this day breathes forth its wrath from within the mountain in clouds of smoke and burning ash.

The war was now triumphantly concluded. The empire of Ngalengkå had fallen. Sintå and Tridjåtå were rescued from the blazing palace. Yet the atmosphere was full of sorrow for those who had fallen. Wibisånå wept bitterly for the dead Kumbåkarnå as he buried him. Then he asked to follow the others on their homeward journey; but instead Råmå appointed him the new King of Ngalengkå and urged him to stay behind and rebuild the devastated kingdom. Sugriwå then departed for his own land, accompanied by the remnants of his army.

Råmå and Sintå were at last reunited after their long separation. Together with Lesmånå and Hanoman they returned home to Ngajodyå, where Baråtå came out to greet them and surrendered the glittering palace to Råmå, who was soon after crowned as Dåsåråtå's rightful heir.

But the unlucky Sintå was to undergo still one last trial. On her return to Ngajodyå she was looked on with suspicion by high and low alike. Was it possible that after so many years in the palace of Ngalengkå Dåsåmukå had not finally had his will of her? To prove her purity, Sintå asked for a great pyre to be prepared and set alight; and this she then solemnly ascended. The flames parted before her, and she emerged radiant and unscathed. Finally vindicated, Sintå rejoined her husband and together they ruled Ngajodyå for many years in great happiness and peace.

# GLOSSARY

*Abangan* (Jav.) Persons or groups who adhere to the traditional Javanese *mélange* of Hindu-Buddhism, animism, and Islamic mysticism, as opposed to the more strait-laced, orthodox *santri* (q.v.).

*Adipati* (Jav.) A King of secondary or subordinate rank.

*Agama Bali* (Ind.) The syncretic religion of Bali.

*Arjå* (Jav.) One of the highest titles of nobility.

*Bambang* (Jav.) A courtesy title for a young *satryå*, generally with the implication that he is still unmarried.

*Batårå* (Jav.) A special title for male deities.

*Begawan* (Jav.) A title given to a religious ascetic of noble origin. It is especially used for kings who have abandoned their thrones to seek religious enlightenment.

*Betari* (Jav.) A special title for female deities. (See *Batårå*)

*Bimå Kunting* (Jav.) Literally "the dwarf Bimå"; this is a favorite nickname for the small but fierce Radèn Setyaki.

*Brahmånå* (Jav.) A member of the *Brahmånå* or priestly caste.

*Bråtåjudå Djåjåbinangun* (Jav.) Literally "the war of the children of Barata in which victory is won"; this is the full Javanese name for the final war between the Kuråwå and the Pendåwå.

*Butå* (Jav.) A general word denoting demon or giant.

*Dahjang* (Jav.) Normally this word means the guardian spirit of a Javanese village. In *wayang* it is a special title conferred on Durnå in recognition of his unsurpassed learning and magical power.

*Dalang* (Jav.) The puppeteer of the *wayang* shadow-play, who sings, jokes, narrates, philosophizes, and manipulates the puppets the whole night through. For Javanese mystics he represents a symbol of the Supreme Being.

*Désa* (Jav.) Peasant, primitive.

*Déwi* (Jav.) The usual title for a princess or other high-born lady.

*Djaman Budå* (Jav.) The pre-Islamic era in Javanese history.

*Durung Djåwå* (Jav.) "Not yet Javanese," i.e., still an irrational child.

*Kalimåsådå* (Jav.) The holy text which is Judistirå's special magical attribute. The name has been interpreted as *Kalimah Sahadat*, the Moslem confession of faith. There is a tradition that before his death Judistirå handed this text to Sunan Kalidjågå, the most eminent of the Islamic proselytizing saints in Java.

*Kasar* (Jav.) Crude, inelegant, rough, impolite.

*Kelir* (Jav.) The white cotton screen, framed first in red cloth and then with wooden beams, against which the puppets are held during a *wayang* performance. When the oil-lamp, or *bléntjong,* is lit, the flickering shadows of the puppets appear on the far side of the *kelir*.

*Kjai* (Jav.) Title of respect, meaning something like "Revered Father." It may be used for both old and wise people and sacred, magically potent objects, such as gongs, *wayang* puppets, *krisses*, and spears.

*Kråmå* (Jav.) The honorific Javanese language of respect used to strangers and persons of higher social rank.

*Kuntå* (Jav.) The name of Karnå's most powerful magical arrow, given to him by his father, Batårå Suryå.

*Kuråwå* (Jav.) The Left faction. Literally the brothers of Kurupati (Sujudånå), but more generally used to describe all Dreståråtå's sons and their allies in the Bråtåjudå.

*Lakon* (Jav.) An episode from the Javanized Ramayana or Mahabharata, serving as the plot for a single night's *wayang* performance.

*Lurah* (Jav.) Usually this term means "village headman," but it can also mean a specific rank at the Javanese courts (often given to talented artists and craftsmen of less than noble (origin) or a title indicating great respect for someone lower in rank than oneself.

*Måhåméru* (Jav.) The World-Mountain, which reaches from Heaven to Earth. At its peak the Gods have their abode. The Javanese identify it with Mount Semeru in East Java.

*Nasib* (Jav.) Fate, destiny.

*Nèm* (Jav.) Young.

*Ngoko* (Jav.) The expressive, pungent Javanese language used towards friends, family, and persons of lower social rank. (See *kråmå*)

*Nijågå* (Jav.) The performers in a Javanese *gamelan* orchestra.

*Oosthoek* (Dutch) The largely Madurese-settled area of East Java that stretches east of Malang to Banjuwangi.

*Ora pantès* (Jav.) Improper, inappropriate, undignified.

*Panditå Ratu* (Jav.) Priest-King, the ideal Javanese rule, who combines religious authority and wisdom with secular power and majesty.

*Påntjånåkå* (Jav.) The name of the razor-sharp, elongated index fingernails of Wrekudårå, Hanoman, and Sang Hyang Baju.

*Pasisir* (Jav.) The North coast of Java, especially the area between Tjirebon and Surabaja. Much more strongly influenced by Islam than the interior, and in far more frequent contact with the outside world, these North coast cities developed a distinctive culture of their own. Historically they have competed with the interior for hegemony over Java.

*Pasopati* (Jav.) The name of Ardjunå's invincible magic arrow.

*Patih* (Jav.) Chief Minister to a King. The Patih is often a man of the lesser nobility, or even from the common people, who has risen to power by sheer ability. His office is purely secular and administrative.

*Pendåwå* (Jav.) The Right faction. A generic term for Judistirå, Wrekudårå, Ardjunå, Nangkulå, and Sadéwå, Pandu's legitimate sons by Kunti and Madrim. Sometimes loosely used to indicate not just the brothers but all their friends and allies as well.

*Pengchianat* (Ind.) A traitor.

*Polèng* (Jav.) A woven cloth with black, red, white, and yellow checks, believed to have special magical properties. In *wayang* it is worn only by Wrekudårå, Hanoman, Sang Hyang Baju, and Déwå Rutji.

*Prabu* (Jav.) The usual title for a King.

*Priangan* The interior plateau of West Java, heartland of the Sundanese ethnic group.

*Punåkawan* (Jav.) Literally "attendants," it has come to mean, in *wayang*, the small group of comic, grotesque male companions of the chief heroes.

*Radèn* (Jav.) Usual title of respect for a man of *satryå* rank.

*Ramé* (Jav.) Noisy.

*Rasekså* (Jav.) Monstrous giant. The traditional enemies of the *satryå* in most *wayang* stories.

*Resi* (Jav.) Religious ascetic and mystical teacher. It appears to have a slightly wider and vaguer significance than *Begawan* (q.v.).

*Saé* (Jav.) Beautiful, good.

*Sang Hyang* (Jav.) Alternative title to *Batårå* (q.v.) for male deities.

*Santri* (Jav.) Persons or groups in Java who adhere strictly to the laws and precepts of Islam. Usually used in contrast to *abangan* (q.v.).

*Satryå* (Jav.) A member of the military-administrative secular ruling class. More generally, anyone who sets out to live by the *satryå* code.

*Semar Påpå* (Jav.) Literally "Semar in Distress," this is the title of one of the most magically powerful *lakons*.

*Sepuh* (Jav.) Old, aged.

*Sétan* (Jav.) A general word for a malevolent, or at least potentially malevolent, spirit.

*Sétrågåndåmaju* (Jav.) Literally "deserted place smelling of corpses," this is the usual Javanese name for the abode of Betari Durgå.

*Sri* (Jav.) A very exalted title, usually reserved for kings.

*Taman Siswå* (Jav.) Literally "Garden of Pupils," the phrase was the name given to the "wild" schools set up by Ki Hadjar Dewantoro in the 1920's in opposition to the colonial Dutch educational system. Ki Hadjar's central idea was to combine Western and Javanese educational concepts in the service of a new humanism.

*Tegal Kurusétrå* (Jav.) The battlefield where the Bråtåjudå Djåjåbinangun takes place. The name means literally "Burial-Field of the Kuråwå."

*Tjåkrå* (Jav.) The magical weapon of Kresnå. It is usually represented iconographically as an arrow tipped with a blazing wheel of fire.

*Tjåndåbiråwå* (Jav.) The magical weapon of Prabu Salyå, given to him by Begawan Bagaspati. When released it takes the form of myriads of dwarfish demons. Any attack on them merely multiplies their number.

*Tjotjog* (Jav.) In harmony with, appropriate.

*Triwikråmå* (Jav.) As a verb this means to assume a terrible, demonic form, generally out of rage.

*Wadat* (Jav.) Celibate.

*Wayang* (Jav.) Literally "shadow," it has come to mean the Javanese shadow-play. It can also refer to the individual puppets.

*Widjåjåkusumå* (Jav.) The magical flower of life, supposedly only to be found on the inhospitable island of Nusa Kembangan, off the south coast of Java.

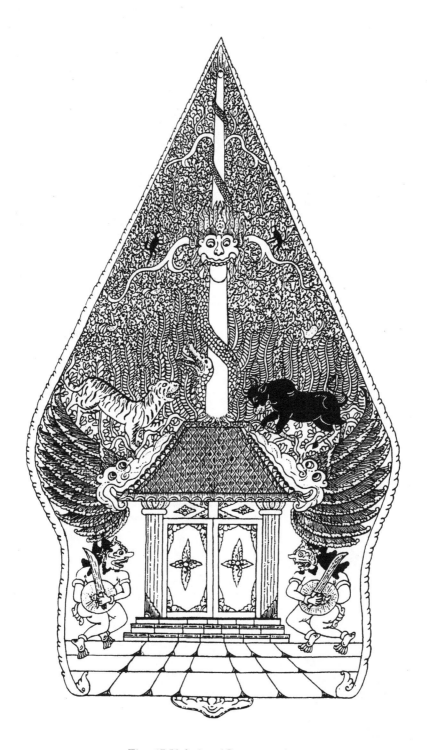

Fig. 65 Kekajon (Gunungan)

CPSIA information can be obtained
at www.ICGtesting.com
Printed in the USA
BVHW091916220720
584343BV00004B/152

9 786028 397937